TEST PREP WORKBOOK

SIDE by SIDE

3

Plus

Steven J. Molinsky • Bill Bliss

Side by Side Plus Test Prep Workbook 3

Pearson Education, 10 Bank Street, White Plains, NY 10606

Staff credits: The people who make up the *Side by Side Plus* team, representing content creation, design, manufacturing, marketing, multimedia, project management, publishing, rights management, and testing are Pietro Alongi, Allen Ascher, Rhea Banker, Elizabeth Barker, Lisa Bayrasli, Elizabeth Carlson, Jennifer Castro, Tracey Munz Cataldo, Diane Cipollone, Aerin Csigay, Victoria Denkus, Dave Dickey, Daniel Dwyer, Wanda España, Oliva Fernandez, Warren Fischbach, Pam Fishman, Nancy Flaggman, Patrice Fraccio, Irene Frankel, Aliza Greenblatt, Lester Holmes, Leslie Johnson, Janet Johnston, Caroline Kasterine, Barry Katzen, Ray Keating, Renee Langan, Jaime Lieber, José Antonio Méndez, Julie Molnar, Alison Pei, Pamela Pia, Stuart Radcliffe, Jennifer Raspiller, Kriston Reinmuth, Mary Perrotta Rich, Tania Saiz-Sousa, Katherine Sullivan, Paula Van Ells, Kenneth Volcjak, Paula Williams, and Wendy Wolf.

Text composition: TSI Graphics, Inc.

Illustrations: Richard E. Hill

The authors gratefully acknowledge the contribution of Tina Carver in the development of the original *Side by Side* program.

ISBN-10: 0-13-418675-3
ISBN-13: 978-0-13-418675-7

Printed in the United States of America

1 2 3 4 5 6 7 8 9 10—V011—23 22 21 20 19 18 17 16

CONTENTS

PREFACE

Side by Side Plus Test Prep Workbook 3 provides unit achievement tests designed to reinforce and assess the learning objectives in *Side by Side Plus Student Book 3*. The tests provide focused coverage of lifeskill competencies and employment topics, assess student progress, and prepare students for the types of standardized tests and performance assessments used by many instructional programs. The content of each test is based on the grammar, vocabulary, and topics covered in the particular unit of the student book.

The achievement tests offer students practice with a variety of test-item formats:

- Multiple-choice questions assess vocabulary, grammar, reading, lifeskill and work-related competencies, and literacy tasks (such as reading classifed ads, signs, and everyday documents).

- Listening assessments offer practice with the types of listening comprehension tasks common in standardized tests.

- Writing assessments can be evaluated using a scoring rubric and collected in portfolios of students' work.

- Speaking performance assessments are designed to stimulate face-to-face interactions between students, for evaluation by the teacher using a standardized scoring rubric, or for self-evaluation by students. (The speaking assessments can also be used to evaluate students individually if time and resources allow for teachers or aides to conduct these assessments on a one-to-one basis.)

Test pages are perforated so that completed tests can be handed in and can serve as a record of students' participation and progress in the instructional program.

The Digital Audio CD included with the Workbook contains all listening activities in the achievement tests. You may choose to do these activities in class or have students complete them on their own using the audio. Listening scripts are provided in *Side by Side Plus Teacher's Guide 3*.

Side by Side Plus Multilevel Activity & Achievement Test Book 3 (included with the Teacher's Guide) provides test preparation strategies, answer keys, scoring rubrics, and resources for documenting students' progress—all in a volume of reproducible masters and an accompanying CD-ROM.

A PERSONAL INFORMATION FORM

Name: (1) _____

Address: (2) _____

City: (3) _____   State: (4) _____   Zip Code: (5) _____

Social Security Number: (6) _____   Country of Origin: (7) _____

Telephone: (8) _____   E-mail: (9) _____   Date of Birth: (10) _____

Height: (11) _____   Eye Color: (12) _____   Hair Color: (13) _____   Marital Status: (14) _____

Family Members in Household (Name—Relationship):

(15) _____

Look at the information. Choose the correct line on the form.

1. 11/14/88
ⓐ Line 5
ⓑ Line 6
ⓒ Line 8
ⓓ Line 10

2. 224-67-8139
ⓐ Line 5
ⓑ Line 6
ⓒ Line 8
ⓓ Line 10

3. Mexico
ⓐ Line 3
ⓑ Line 4
ⓒ Line 7
ⓓ Line 10

4. 1263 Main St.
ⓐ Line 2
ⓑ Line 7
ⓒ Line 9
ⓓ Line 15

5. 5'9"
ⓐ Line 5
ⓑ Line 6
ⓒ Line 10
ⓓ Line 11

6. married
ⓐ Line 7
ⓑ Line 12
ⓒ Line 14
ⓓ Line 15

7. FL
ⓐ Line 3
ⓑ Line 4
ⓒ Line 5
ⓓ Line 14

8. blue
ⓐ Line 11
ⓑ Line 12
ⓒ Line 13
ⓓ Line 14

9. (305) 965-4213
ⓐ Line 5
ⓑ Line 6
ⓒ Line 8
ⓓ Line 9

10. Alma Suarez—wife
ⓐ Line 1
ⓑ Line 2
ⓒ Line 14
ⓓ Line 15

11. Miami
ⓐ Line 3
ⓑ Line 4
ⓒ Line 5
ⓓ Line 9

12. cjs24@msl.com
ⓐ Line 2
ⓑ Line 3
ⓒ Line 8
ⓓ Line 9

1 ⓐ ⓑ ⓒ ⓓ   4 ⓐ ⓑ ⓒ ⓓ   7 ⓐ ⓑ ⓒ ⓓ   10 ⓐ ⓑ ⓒ ⓓ

2 ⓐ ⓑ ⓒ ⓓ   5 ⓐ ⓑ ⓒ ⓓ   8 ⓐ ⓑ ⓒ ⓓ   11 ⓐ ⓑ ⓒ ⓓ

3 ⓐ ⓑ ⓒ ⓓ   6 ⓐ ⓑ ⓒ ⓓ   9 ⓐ ⓑ ⓒ ⓓ   12 ⓐ ⓑ ⓒ ⓓ

Go to the next page ⟩ **1**

B GRAMMAR IN CONTEXT: Small Talk at Work

Choose the correct answer to complete the conversations.

13. What are you _____?
- (A) reading
- (B) looking
- (C) read
- (D) look

14. _____ a book about the president.
- (A) I read
- (B) I'm reading
- (C) I watch
- (D) I'm watching

15. Do you _____ biographies?
- (A) reading
- (B) like to
- (C) like to read
- (D) liking

16. Yes. _____ them whenever I can.
- (A) I read
- (B) I'm reading
- (C) I like
- (D) I like to

17. _____ swim?
- (A) You like
- (B) You like to
- (C) You do like to
- (D) Do you like to

18. No. _____ a very good swimmer.
- (A) I don't
- (B) I'm not
- (C) You're
- (D) You aren't

19. _____ exercise?
- (A) You often
- (B) How often you
- (C) How often do you
- (D) Do you how often

20. I exercise _____.
- (A) three times
- (B) three times a week
- (C) three weeks
- (D) every

21. What do you like to do _____?
- (A) in your free time
- (B) in your time
- (C) in your free
- (D) when your free time

22. I like to _____.
- (A) tennis player
- (B) tennis
- (C) playing tennis
- (D) play tennis

. . . .

13 (A) (B) (C) (D)   16 (A) (B) (C) (D)   19 (A) (B) (C) (D)   21 (A) (B) (C) (D)

14 (A) (B) (C) (D)   17 (A) (B) (C) (D)   20 (A) (B) (C) (D)   22 (A) (B) (C) (D)

15 (A) (B) (C) (D)   18 (A) (B) (C) (D)

Go to the next page ⇒

C CLOZE READING: Grading Systems

Choose the correct answers to complete the paragraph.

There [am (A)] [is (B)] [are ●] different types of grading systems [out (A)] [in (B)] [between (C)] [23] different schools. Some schools [use (A)] [uses (B)] [using (C)] [24] a letter marking system with the letters A, B, C, D, [between (A)] [and (B)] [for (C)] [25] F. [Other (A)] [Others (B)] [Another (C)] [26] schools use the letters E, G, F, and P to describe students as Excellent, [Grade (A)] [Get (B)] [Good (C)] [27], Fair, or [Pretty (A)] [Popular (B)] [Poor (C)] [28]. Some schools [don't (A)] [doesn't (B)] [aren't (C)] [29] use letter grades. They use [number (A)] [numbers (B)] [names (C)] [30] such as 75%, 80%, 85% or they don't use grades at all.

D READING: The Education System

Look at the table. Choose the correct answer.

Here is a table that shows the levels of high school and college in the education system in the United States. Notice that we use the same words to describe the levels of students in both parts of the education system. Study the table. Then do Numbers 31 through 34.

HIGH SCHOOL GRADE	LEVEL	YEAR OF COLLEGE
9	Freshman	1
10	Sophomore	2
11	Junior	3
12	Senior	4

31. Carla is a junior in high school. What grade is she in?
    - (A) Grade 9.
    - (B) Grade 10.
    - (C) Grade 11.
    - (D) Grade 12.

32. Martin is in his last year as a student at Carleton College. Which sentence is correct?
    - (A) He's in Grade 9.
    - (B) He's a freshman.
    - (C) He's in Grade 12.
    - (D) He's a senior.

33. Wendy is a sophomore. She's 20 years old. Which sentence is probably true?
    - (A) Wendy goes to high school.
    - (B) Wendy goes to college.
    - (C) Wendy is in the 10th grade.
    - (D) Wendy was a junior last year.

34. The paragraph describes two parts of the education system. What is another part of the education system that isn't described in the paragraph?
    - (A) Elementary schools.
    - (B) High schools.
    - (C) Colleges.
    - (D) Supermarkets.

23 (A) (B) (C) (D)   26 (A) (B) (C) (D)   29 (A) (B) (C) (D)   32 (A) (B) (C) (D)
24 (A) (B) (C) (D)   27 (A) (B) (C) (D)   30 (A) (B) (C) (D)   33 (A) (B) (C) (D)
25 (A) (B) (C) (D)   28 (A) (B) (C) (D)   31 (A) (B) (C) (D)   34 (A) (B) (C) (D)

Go to the next page ⟹

3

E LISTENING ASSESSMENT: An Automated Message

Read and listen to the questions. Then listen to the automated telephone message and answer the questions.

35. How can you listen to the information in Spanish?
- (A) Press 1.
- (B) Press 2.
- (C) Press 3.
- (D) Press 4.

36. How can you listen to the information in Arabic?
- (A) Press 4.
- (B) Press 5.
- (C) Press 6.
- (D) Press 7.

37. How many days a week is the program open?
- (A) Two.
- (B) Three.
- (C) Five.
- (D) Seven.

38. When can you take a placement test for fall English classes?
- (A) August 26.
- (B) September 3.
- (C) September 10.
- (D) September 26.

39. On what date do fall classes begin?
- (A) September 2.
- (B) September 3.
- (C) September 10.
- (D) 8:30 A.M.

40. How can you listen to the information again?
- (A) Press 1.
- (B) Press S.
- (C) Press #.
- (D) Press *.

F WRITING ASSESSMENT: A Personal Information Form

Name: _____

Address: _____

City: _____ State: _____ Zip Code: _____

Social Security Number: _____ Country of Origin: _____

Telephone: _____ E-mail: _____ Date of Birth: _____

Height: _____ Eye Color: _____ Hair Color: _____ Marital Status: _____

Family Members in Household (Name—Relationship):

_____ _____

_____ _____

G SPEAKING ASSESSMENT

I can ask and answer these questions:

Ask Answer
- ☐ ☐ Where are you from?
- ☐ ☐ Where do you live now?
- ☐ ☐ Are you married?
- ☐ ☐ Are you single?

Ask Answer
- ☐ ☐ Who are the people in your family?
- ☐ ☐ Do you work or go to school?
- ☐ ☐ What do you do/study?
- ☐ ☐ What do you like to do in your free time?

35 Ⓐ Ⓑ Ⓒ Ⓓ   37 Ⓐ Ⓑ Ⓒ Ⓓ   39 Ⓐ Ⓑ Ⓒ Ⓓ

36 Ⓐ Ⓑ Ⓒ Ⓓ   38 Ⓐ Ⓑ Ⓒ Ⓓ   40 Ⓐ Ⓑ Ⓒ Ⓓ

STOP

A SMALL TALK ABOUT PAST EVENTS

Choose the correct answer.

Example:

My children _____ sick yesterday.
- (A) are
- (B) is
- (C) was
- ● were

1. Traffic _____ very bad this morning.
   - (A) are
   - (B) be
   - (C) was
   - (D) were

2. I _____ a movie last night.
   - (A) go
   - (B) went
   - (C) see
   - (D) saw

3. I _____ sleep well last night.
   - (A) don't
   - (B) didn't
   - (C) am not
   - (D) doesn't

4. Did you _____ today?
   - (A) the bus
   - (B) bus to work
   - (C) take the bus
   - (D) took the bus

5. What _____ last weekend?
   - (A) did you do
   - (B) do you did
   - (C) you do
   - (D) you did

6. Our supervisor _____ very angry this morning.
   - (A) did
   - (B) was
   - (C) be
   - (D) were

7. _____ you nervous while the boss was visiting our department?
   - (A) Are
   - (B) Will
   - (C) Was
   - (D) Were

8. _____ a good vacation?
   - (A) You had
   - (B) Did you had
   - (C) Did you have
   - (D) Had you

9. I _____ an accident while I _____ to work today.
   - (A) see . . . was driving
   - (B) saw . . . was driving
   - (C) saw . . . am driving
   - (D) was seeing . . . drove

1 (A) (B) (C) (D)   4 (A) (B) (C) (D)   7 (A) (B) (C) (D)

2 (A) (B) (C) (D)   5 (A) (B) (C) (D)   8 (A) (B) (C) (D)

3 (A) (B) (C) (D)   6 (A) (B) (C) (D)   9 (A) (B) (C) (D)

Go to the next page

Choose the correct answer to complete the conversations.

Ex: _____ I arrived late this morning.
- Ⓐ I sorry
- ● I'm sorry
- Ⓒ You sorry
- Ⓓ You're sorry

10. What _____?
- Ⓐ happen
- Ⓑ happens
- Ⓒ happening
- Ⓓ happened

11. My car _____ while I was driving to work.
- Ⓐ broke down
- Ⓑ break down
- Ⓒ breaks down
- Ⓓ breaking down

12. _____ bad.
- Ⓐ You
- Ⓑ You're too
- Ⓒ That's too
- Ⓓ That

13. I want to _____.
- Ⓐ apology
- Ⓑ apologize
- Ⓒ apologizing
- Ⓓ sorry

14. For _____?
- Ⓐ what
- Ⓑ when
- Ⓒ why
- Ⓓ how

15. I _____ finish my work today.
- Ⓐ do
- Ⓑ did
- Ⓒ could
- Ⓓ couldn't

16. _____ not?
- Ⓐ You're
- Ⓑ Who
- Ⓒ What
- Ⓓ Why

17. I hurt _____ while I was moving some boxes.
- Ⓐ myself
- Ⓑ me
- Ⓒ you
- Ⓓ back

18. _____ to hear that. Are you okay?
- Ⓐ You're sorry
- Ⓑ I'm sorry
- Ⓒ I'm glad
- Ⓓ You're glad

Yes. I'm okay.

Good.

10 Ⓐ Ⓑ Ⓒ Ⓓ   13 Ⓐ Ⓑ Ⓒ Ⓓ   16 Ⓐ Ⓑ Ⓒ Ⓓ

11 Ⓐ Ⓑ Ⓒ Ⓓ   14 Ⓐ Ⓑ Ⓒ Ⓓ   17 Ⓐ Ⓑ Ⓒ Ⓓ

12 Ⓐ Ⓑ Ⓒ Ⓓ   15 Ⓐ Ⓑ Ⓒ Ⓓ   18 Ⓐ Ⓑ Ⓒ Ⓓ

Go to the next page ⟩

C GRAMMAR IN CONTEXT: Oral Directions to Places; Clarification Strategies

Choose the correct answer to complete the conversations.

Ex: Excuse me. _____ the post office?
- Ⓐ Can I get
- Ⓑ Where can I
- Ⓒ How can
- ⬤ How can I get to

19. Walk to the end of this block and _____ right.
- Ⓐ make
- Ⓑ have
- Ⓒ turn
- Ⓓ get

20. Can you tell me _____ Garden Street?
- Ⓐ how to get
- Ⓑ how to get to
- Ⓒ how you go
- Ⓓ how I go

21. Go _____ one block, turn left, and then _____ your second right.
- Ⓐ straight . . . make
- Ⓑ straight . . . turn
- Ⓒ street . . . take
- Ⓓ street . . . turn

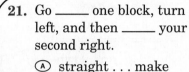

22. Straight, left, and then the second _____ ?
- Ⓐ take
- Ⓑ straight
- Ⓒ left
- Ⓓ right

23. Yes. _____
- Ⓐ I'm correct.
- Ⓑ You're wrong.
- Ⓒ That's correct.
- Ⓓ That's incorrect.

24. Take Bus Number 7 and _____ at Lake Street.
- Ⓐ take off
- Ⓑ get on
- Ⓒ get off
- Ⓓ take on

25. _____ Bus Number 11?
- Ⓐ Did you say
- Ⓑ You say
- Ⓒ Do you say
- Ⓓ Did I say

26. _____ Number 7.
- Ⓐ Yes.
- Ⓑ No.
- Ⓒ Maybe.
- Ⓓ You say.

27. And _____ should I get off?
- Ⓐ who
- Ⓑ why
- Ⓒ how
- Ⓓ where

At Lake Street.

Thank you.

. . . .

19 Ⓐ Ⓑ Ⓒ Ⓓ   22 Ⓐ Ⓑ Ⓒ Ⓓ   25 Ⓐ Ⓑ Ⓒ Ⓓ

20 Ⓐ Ⓑ Ⓒ Ⓓ   23 Ⓐ Ⓑ Ⓒ Ⓓ   26 Ⓐ Ⓑ Ⓒ Ⓓ

21 Ⓐ Ⓑ Ⓒ Ⓓ   24 Ⓐ Ⓑ Ⓒ Ⓓ   27 Ⓐ Ⓑ Ⓒ Ⓓ

Go to the next page

Here is part of an accident report that describes an accident between two motor vehicles. Study the diagram and read the statement. Then do Numbers 28 through 31.

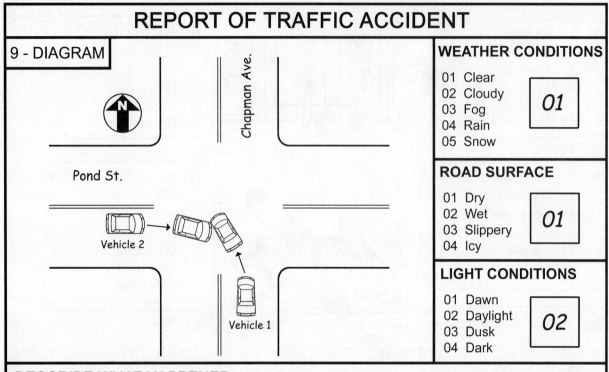

REPORT OF TRAFFIC ACCIDENT

9 - DIAGRAM

Chapman Ave.

Pond St.

N

Vehicle 2

Vehicle 1

WEATHER CONDITIONS

01 Clear
02 Cloudy
03 Fog
04 Rain
05 Snow

01

ROAD SURFACE

01 Dry
02 Wet
03 Slippery
04 Icy

01

LIGHT CONDITIONS

01 Dawn
02 Daylight
03 Dusk
04 Dark

02

DESCRIBE WHAT HAPPENED:

I was driving north on Chapman Avenue. Vehicle 2 was going east on Pond Street. While I was making a left turn onto Pond Street, the driver of Vehicle 2 didn't stop at the Stop sign and hit the front left side of my car.

28. Where did this accident happen?
　Ⓐ On Pond Street.
　Ⓑ On Chapman Avenue.
　Ⓒ While Vehicle 1 was turning left.
　Ⓓ At the intersection of Pond and Chapman.

29. Where did Vehicle 2 hit Vehicle 1?
　Ⓐ At the front right side.
　Ⓑ At the back right side.
　Ⓒ At the driver's side in the front.
　Ⓓ At the driver's side in the back.

30. Where did the driver of Vehicle 1 want to go?
　Ⓐ West on Pond Street.
　Ⓑ East on Pond Street.
　Ⓒ North on Pond Street.
　Ⓓ South on Chapman Avenue.

31. When the police officer arrived, which driver probably received a ticket for a traffic violation?
　Ⓐ The driver of Vehicle 1.
　Ⓑ The driver of Vehicle 2.
　Ⓒ Both drivers.
　Ⓓ Neither driver.

28 Ⓐ Ⓑ Ⓒ Ⓓ　　30 Ⓐ Ⓑ Ⓒ Ⓓ

29 Ⓐ Ⓑ Ⓒ Ⓓ　　31 Ⓐ Ⓑ Ⓒ Ⓓ

E CLOZE READING: Traffic

Choose the correct answers to complete the story.

I [arrived ● / get ⒝ / go ⒞] at work late yesterday. I usually [drove ⒜ / drive ⒝ / went ⒞] ³² on the Jackson Parkway to get to work, but there was bad [cars ⒜ / slow ⒝ / traffic ⒞] ³³ on the parkway yesterday. Instead, I [drive ⒜ / drove ⒝ / take ⒞] ³⁴ to work on Central Avenue. Unfortunately, there was a bad [accident ⒜ / traffic ⒝ / road ⒞] ³⁵ on Central Avenue. Traffic [doesn't ⒜ / didn't ⒝ / isn't ⒞] ³⁶ move for about an hour [where ⒜ / who ⒝ / while ⒞] ³⁷ the police helped the people in the accident.

F LISTENING ASSESSMENT: Following Directions to a Place

Read and listen to the questions. Then listen to the telephone conversation and answer the questions.

38. What is Rosa's address?
    - Ⓐ 4013 Lake Street.
    - Ⓑ 1430 Lake Street.
    - Ⓒ 1430 Madison Street.
    - Ⓓ 4013 Madison Street.

39. Where is David during this conversation?
    - Ⓐ On Bus Number 5.
    - Ⓑ At Rosa's party.
    - Ⓒ At the post office.
    - Ⓓ At an intersection.

40. Why did David get lost?
    - Ⓐ He took the wrong bus.
    - Ⓑ He got off the bus at the wrong street.
    - Ⓒ He walked the wrong way on Lake Street.
    - Ⓓ He walked the wrong way on Madison Street.

G LEARNING SKILL: Listing Events in Chronological Order

Put the events in order.

_____ I worked in my office all morning.

_____ I went home at 6 P.M.

_____ I went to a meeting in the afternoon.

__1__ I got dressed and had breakfast.

_____ I had lunch at noon.

_____ I took the bus to work.

· ·

32 Ⓐ Ⓑ Ⓒ Ⓓ   35 Ⓐ Ⓑ Ⓒ Ⓓ   38 Ⓐ Ⓑ Ⓒ Ⓓ

33 Ⓐ Ⓑ Ⓒ Ⓓ   36 Ⓐ Ⓑ Ⓒ Ⓓ   39 Ⓐ Ⓑ Ⓒ Ⓓ

34 Ⓐ Ⓑ Ⓒ Ⓓ   37 Ⓐ Ⓑ Ⓒ Ⓓ   40 Ⓐ Ⓑ Ⓒ Ⓓ

Go to the next page ⟹

H WRITING ASSESSMENT: A Traffic Accident Report Form

Imagine that you and another student were in a traffic accident. You were driving Vehicle 1. The other student was driving Vehicle 2. Work together to decide what happened and where. Then work separately to draw a diagram and write a statement about the accident. Finally, exchange information to complete the accident report.

REPORT OF TRAFFIC ACCIDENT

DIAGRAM (Draw a diagram of what happened.)

WEATHER CONDITIONS	ROAD SURFACE	LIGHT CONDITIONS
01 Clear	01 Dry	01 Dawn
02 Cloudy	02 Wet	02 Daylight
03 Fog	03 Slippery	03 Dusk
04 Rain	04 Icy	04 Dark
05 Snow		

DESCRIBE WHAT HAPPENED:

I SPEAKING ASSESSMENT

I can ask and answer these questions:

Ask Answer
☐ ☐ What did you do yesterday?
☐ ☐ What did you do last weekend?

Ask Answer
☐ ☐ How did you get to school today?
☐ ☐ How can I get to your home from here?

STOP

A COMMUNICATING WITH SCHOOL PERSONNEL

Choose the correct answer.

1. _____ will the parents' meeting start this evening?
   - Ⓐ What day
   - Ⓑ What time
   - Ⓒ What day is it
   - Ⓓ What time is it

2. _____ give this note to my daughter's teacher?
   - Ⓐ You will
   - Ⓑ Please you will
   - Ⓒ You will please
   - Ⓓ Will you please

3. I promise _____ my daughter with her homework.
   - Ⓐ help
   - Ⓑ you help
   - Ⓒ I'll help
   - Ⓓ you'll help

4. _____ school tomorrow?
   - Ⓐ Will there be
   - Ⓑ Will be
   - Ⓒ Will open
   - Ⓓ Will be open

5. Could I _____ a pencil to fill out this form?
   - Ⓐ has
   - Ⓑ give
   - Ⓒ borrow
   - Ⓓ lend

6. Would you _____ me a textbook during the summer so I can help my son with math?
   - Ⓐ take
   - Ⓑ lend
   - Ⓒ read
   - Ⓓ borrow

7. Is Anthony _____ fail math this year?
   - Ⓐ going
   - Ⓑ going to
   - Ⓒ will
   - Ⓓ will be

8. _____ help me fill out this registration form?
   - Ⓐ Could you
   - Ⓑ Could I
   - Ⓒ Will I
   - Ⓓ Would we

9. _____ is my daughter doing in your class?
   - Ⓐ Why
   - Ⓑ When
   - Ⓒ Where
   - Ⓓ How

10. In my _____, the students aren't getting enough homework.
    - Ⓐ think
    - Ⓑ thinks
    - Ⓒ opinion
    - Ⓓ I think

11. My son _____ be in school tomorrow. _____ absent.
    - Ⓐ will . . . He's
    - Ⓑ will . . . He'll be
    - Ⓒ won't . . . He's
    - Ⓓ won't . . . He'll be

12. I think my son _____ doing his homework well because he _____ understand the assignments.
    - Ⓐ is . . . doesn't
    - Ⓑ isn't . . . doesn't
    - Ⓒ is . . . don't
    - Ⓓ isn't . . . does

. . . .

1 Ⓐ Ⓑ Ⓒ Ⓓ   4 Ⓐ Ⓑ Ⓒ Ⓓ   7 Ⓐ Ⓑ Ⓒ Ⓓ   10 Ⓐ Ⓑ Ⓒ Ⓓ

2 Ⓐ Ⓑ Ⓒ Ⓓ   5 Ⓐ Ⓑ Ⓒ Ⓓ   8 Ⓐ Ⓑ Ⓒ Ⓓ   11 Ⓐ Ⓑ Ⓒ Ⓓ

3 Ⓐ Ⓑ Ⓒ Ⓓ   6 Ⓐ Ⓑ Ⓒ Ⓓ   9 Ⓐ Ⓑ Ⓒ Ⓓ   12 Ⓐ Ⓑ Ⓒ Ⓓ

B GRAMMAR IN CONTEXT: Communicating with School Personnel—Reporting an Absence & Making an Appointment

Choose the correct answer to complete the conversations.

Good morning. Franklin Elementary School.

Yes, Mr. Chen?

15. What's _____ teacher's name?
- (A) my
- (B) your
- (C) her
- (D) his

13. Hello. _____ Peter Chen.
- (A) This is
- (B) I
- (C) You
- (D) You are

14. My son, Jason, is sick. He'll be _____ today.
- (A) a clinic
- (B) a doctor
- (C) absent
- (D) present

16. He's in Mrs. Tyler's _____ class.
- (A) four
- (B) fourth grade
- (C) grade
- (D) room

17. Hello. This is Sonia Belkin. I'd like to _____ with the principal.
- (A) make an appointment
- (B) appoint
- (C) appointment
- (D) meeting

19. No. _____ working. How about the day after tomorrow?
- (A) You're
- (B) I
- (C) I'll
- (D) I'll be

21. Can I _____ with him next Monday morning?
- (A) meet
- (B) meeting
- (C) appoint
- (D) appointment

Yes. Thank you.

18. Yes, Mrs. Belkin. Can you _____ tomorrow at 9 A.M.?
- (A) go
- (B) go out
- (C) come in
- (D) appointment

20. I'm sorry. Mr. Price _____ be here. _____ at a meeting.
- (A) will . . . He'll be
- (B) won't . . . He'll be
- (C) will . . . He'll
- (D) won't . . . He'll

22. Yes. _____ 10:00 okay?
- (A) Will
- (B) Be
- (C) Meet
- (D) Is

See you Monday, Mrs. Belkin.

. . . .

13 (A) (B) (C) (D)   16 (A) (B) (C) (D)   19 (A) (B) (C) (D)   21 (A) (B) (C) (D)

14 (A) (B) (C) (D)   17 (A) (B) (C) (D)   20 (A) (B) (C) (D)   22 (A) (B) (C) (D)

15 (A) (B) (C) (D)   18 (A) (B) (C) (D)

Go to the next page

C READING: A School Diagram

Here is a diagram of one floor of a high school. Study the diagram. Then do Numbers 23 through 30.

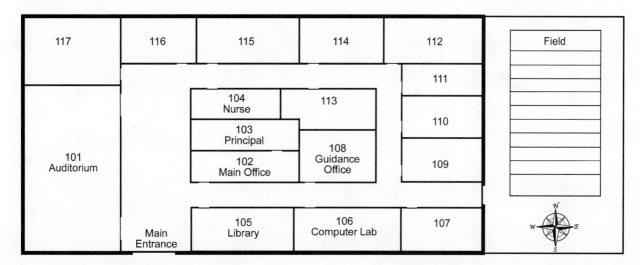

23. What's across from the main office?
    - Ⓐ The gym.
    - Ⓑ The guidance office.
    - Ⓒ The library.
    - Ⓓ The computer lab.

24. The music classroom is behind the auditorium. What's the music teacher's room number?
    - Ⓐ 114.
    - Ⓑ 115.
    - Ⓒ 116.
    - Ⓓ 117.

25. Where is the school's field?
    - Ⓐ On the east side.
    - Ⓑ On the west side.
    - Ⓒ On the south side.
    - Ⓓ On the north side.

26. Irene needs advice about her college applications. Where is she probably going?
    - Ⓐ To Room 102.
    - Ⓑ To Room 105.
    - Ⓒ To Room 106.
    - Ⓓ To Room 108.

27. Carlos doesn't feel well. Where is he probably going?
    - Ⓐ To Room 104.
    - Ⓑ To Room 103.
    - Ⓒ To Room 102.
    - Ⓓ To Room 101.

28. The cafeteria in this school is in Room 10. Where is it probably located?
    - Ⓐ In the auditorium.
    - Ⓑ In the basement.
    - Ⓒ On the first floor.
    - Ⓓ On the second floor.

29. Ms. Martin's classroom is Room Number 233. Where is it probably located?
    - Ⓐ In the basement.
    - Ⓑ On the first floor.
    - Ⓒ On the second floor.
    - Ⓓ On the third floor.

30. Which of these classrooms probably doesn't have any windows?
    - Ⓐ Room 109.
    - Ⓑ Room 111.
    - Ⓒ Room 113.
    - Ⓓ Room 115.

. . . .

23 Ⓐ Ⓑ Ⓒ Ⓓ   25 Ⓐ Ⓑ Ⓒ Ⓓ   27 Ⓐ Ⓑ Ⓒ Ⓓ   29 Ⓐ Ⓑ Ⓒ Ⓓ

24 Ⓐ Ⓑ Ⓒ Ⓓ   26 Ⓐ Ⓑ Ⓒ Ⓓ   28 Ⓐ Ⓑ Ⓒ Ⓓ   30 Ⓐ Ⓑ Ⓒ Ⓓ

Go to the next page ⟶

D CLOZE READING: A Note to School

Choose the correct answers to complete the note.

Dare Dear Deer Ms. Watson,
(A) ● (C)

Your Her My ³¹daughter, Victoria, won't will not ³²be in school tomorrow
(A) (B) (C)   (A) (B) (C)

morning. She She'll She's ³³be at the doctor's office. She have has to has ³⁴an
(A) (B) (C)   (A) (B) (C)

appointment at 9:30. I I'll She'll ³⁵bring her to school during after for ³⁶the
(A) (B) (C)   (A) (B) (C)

appointment.

Sincerely Dear Thank ³⁷,
(A) (B) (C)

Lydia Petrero

E LISTENING ASSESSMENT: Communicating with School Personnel

Read and listen to the questions. Then listen to the telephone conversation and answer the questions.

38. Who is sick?
- (A) Raymond Vacano.
- (B) Mrs. Vacano.
- (C) The school nurse.
- (D) The gym teacher.

39. Where is the student now?
- (A) At home.
- (B) In the gym.
- (C) In the main office.
- (D) In the nurse's office.

40. Where should the mother go?
- (A) To the gym.
- (B) To the hospital.
- (C) To the nurse's office.
- (D) To the main office.

F WRITING ASSESSMENT: A Note to a Teacher

Write a note to your teacher. Explain why you will be absent during your next English class. (Use a separate sheet of paper.)

G SPEAKING ASSESSMENT: Small Talk about Weekend Plans

I can ask and answer these questions:

Ask Answer
- ☐ ☐ What are you going to do this Saturday?
- ☐ ☐ What are you going to do this Sunday?
- ☐ ☐ What's the weather forecast for the weekend?

31 (A) (B) (C) (D)   34 (A) (B) (C) (D)   37 (A) (B) (C) (D)   39 (A) (B) (C) (D)

32 (A) (B) (C) (D)   35 (A) (B) (C) (D)   38 (A) (B) (C) (D)   40 (A) (B) (C) (D)

33 (A) (B) (C) (D)   36 (A) (B) (C) (D)

STOP

A ASKING & ANSWERING TYPICAL JOB INTERVIEW QUESTIONS

Choose the correct answer.

1. Do you know how to _____ a bus?
   - Ⓐ drive
   - Ⓑ drives
   - Ⓒ drove
   - Ⓓ driven

2. I've _____ reports for many years.
   - Ⓐ write
   - Ⓑ writes
   - Ⓒ wrote
   - Ⓓ written

3. Have you ever _____ a presentation?
   - Ⓐ give
   - Ⓑ given
   - Ⓒ gave
   - Ⓓ gives

4. _____ you able to work weekends?
   - Ⓐ Was
   - Ⓑ Do
   - Ⓒ Are
   - Ⓓ Can

5. I know how to _____ inventory.
   - Ⓐ took
   - Ⓑ take
   - Ⓒ taken
   - Ⓓ takes

6. Have you ever _____ arrested?
   - Ⓐ is
   - Ⓑ was
   - Ⓒ be
   - Ⓓ been

7. I can _____ three languages.
   - Ⓐ speak
   - Ⓑ spoke
   - Ⓒ speaks
   - Ⓓ spoken

8. I _____ a computer class last year.
   - Ⓐ take
   - Ⓑ takes
   - Ⓒ took
   - Ⓓ taken

9. What _____ you do in your previous job?
   - Ⓐ do
   - Ⓑ did
   - Ⓒ does
   - Ⓓ done

10. Have you ever _____ a truck?
    - Ⓐ drive
    - Ⓑ drove
    - Ⓒ drives
    - Ⓓ driven

B SMALL TALK ABOUT LEISURE ACTIVITIES

11. A. Have you ever _____ skiing?
    B. Yes. I _____ skiing last year.
    - Ⓐ went . . . go
    - Ⓑ went . . . went
    - Ⓒ gone . . . went
    - Ⓓ go . . . went

12. A. Have you _____ the new Harry Potter movie yet?
    B. Yes. I _____ it last weekend.
    - Ⓐ seen . . . saw
    - Ⓑ saw . . . saw
    - Ⓒ see . . . seen
    - Ⓓ seen . . . see

13. A. I _____ to the mountains last Sunday.
    B. I've never _____ to the mountains.
    - Ⓐ driven . . . drove
    - Ⓑ driven . . . driven
    - Ⓒ drove . . . drove
    - Ⓓ drove . . . driven

14. A. Are you going to _____ today?
    B. No. I've already _____ this week.
    - Ⓐ swim . . . swam
    - Ⓑ swim . . . swum
    - Ⓒ swum . . . swum
    - Ⓓ swam . . . swim

1 Ⓐ Ⓑ Ⓒ Ⓓ 5 Ⓐ Ⓑ Ⓒ Ⓓ 9 Ⓐ Ⓑ Ⓒ Ⓓ 13 Ⓐ Ⓑ Ⓒ Ⓓ
2 Ⓐ Ⓑ Ⓒ Ⓓ 6 Ⓐ Ⓑ Ⓒ Ⓓ 10 Ⓐ Ⓑ Ⓒ Ⓓ 14 Ⓐ Ⓑ Ⓒ Ⓓ
3 Ⓐ Ⓑ Ⓒ Ⓓ 7 Ⓐ Ⓑ Ⓒ Ⓓ 11 Ⓐ Ⓑ Ⓒ Ⓓ
4 Ⓐ Ⓑ Ⓒ Ⓓ 8 Ⓐ Ⓑ Ⓒ Ⓓ 12 Ⓐ Ⓑ Ⓒ Ⓓ

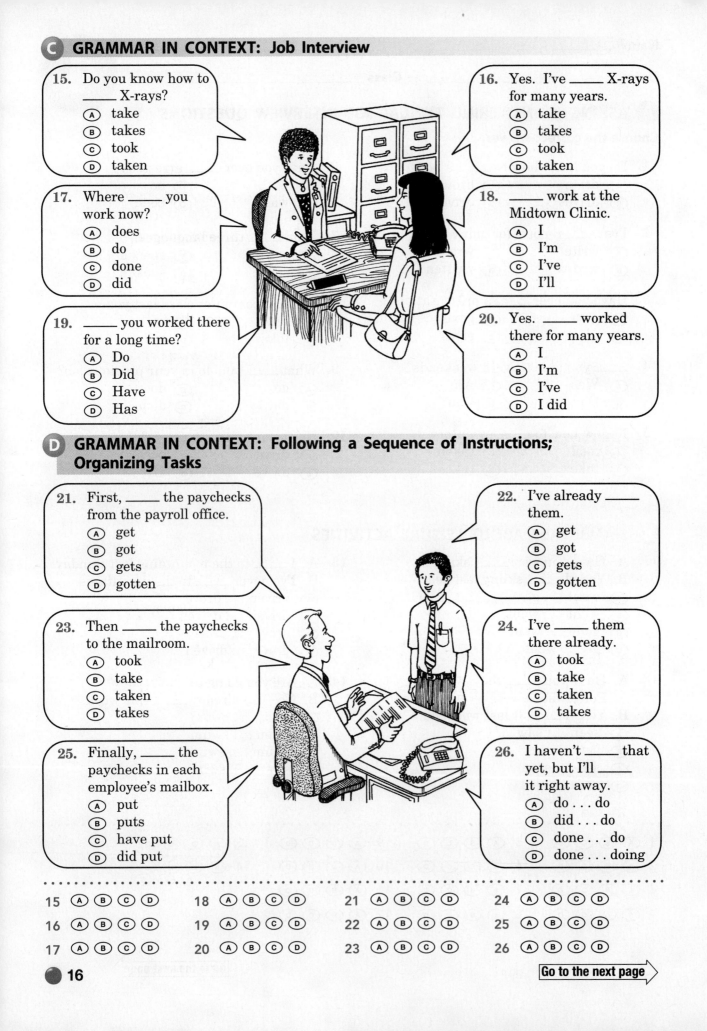

15. Do you know how to _____ X-rays?
   - Ⓐ take
   - Ⓑ takes
   - Ⓒ took
   - Ⓓ taken

16. Yes. I've _____ X-rays for many years.
   - Ⓐ take
   - Ⓑ takes
   - Ⓒ took
   - Ⓓ taken

17. Where _____ you work now?
   - Ⓐ does
   - Ⓑ do
   - Ⓒ done
   - Ⓓ did

18. _____ work at the Midtown Clinic.
   - Ⓐ I
   - Ⓑ I'm
   - Ⓒ I've
   - Ⓓ I'll

19. _____ you worked there for a long time?
   - Ⓐ Do
   - Ⓑ Did
   - Ⓒ Have
   - Ⓓ Has

20. Yes. _____ worked there for many years.
   - Ⓐ I
   - Ⓑ I'm
   - Ⓒ I've
   - Ⓓ I did

D **GRAMMAR IN CONTEXT: Following a Sequence of Instructions; Organizing Tasks**

21. First, _____ the paychecks from the payroll office.
   - Ⓐ get
   - Ⓑ got
   - Ⓒ gets
   - Ⓓ gotten

22. I've already _____ them.
   - Ⓐ get
   - Ⓑ got
   - Ⓒ gets
   - Ⓓ gotten

23. Then _____ the paychecks to the mailroom.
   - Ⓐ took
   - Ⓑ take
   - Ⓒ taken
   - Ⓓ takes

24. I've _____ them there already.
   - Ⓐ took
   - Ⓑ take
   - Ⓒ taken
   - Ⓓ takes

25. Finally, _____ the paychecks in each employee's mailbox.
   - Ⓐ put
   - Ⓑ puts
   - Ⓒ have put
   - Ⓓ did put

26. I haven't _____ that yet, but I'll _____ it right away.
   - Ⓐ do . . . do
   - Ⓑ did . . . do
   - Ⓒ done . . . do
   - Ⓓ done . . . doing

. . . .

15 Ⓐ Ⓑ Ⓒ Ⓓ   18 Ⓐ Ⓑ Ⓒ Ⓓ   21 Ⓐ Ⓑ Ⓒ Ⓓ   24 Ⓐ Ⓑ Ⓒ Ⓓ

16 Ⓐ Ⓑ Ⓒ Ⓓ   19 Ⓐ Ⓑ Ⓒ Ⓓ   22 Ⓐ Ⓑ Ⓒ Ⓓ   25 Ⓐ Ⓑ Ⓒ Ⓓ

17 Ⓐ Ⓑ Ⓒ Ⓓ   20 Ⓐ Ⓑ Ⓒ Ⓓ   23 Ⓐ Ⓑ Ⓒ Ⓓ   26 Ⓐ Ⓑ Ⓒ Ⓓ

Go to the next page ⟩

E CLOZE READING: Employment Application Procedures

Choose the correct answers to complete the story.

I've completed my job [applying(A) application(●) employer(C)] form. I've filled in all my personal

[application(A) vocation(B) information(C)] 27. I've stated the [position(A) company(B) employee(C)] 28

I'm applying for. I've listed my high school and college in the [work(A) education(B) application(C)] 29

history. I've listed my [now(A) today(B) current(C)] 30 and former jobs. I've written my

[days(A) dates(B) schedules(C)] 31 of employment for each position. I've written the name and address

of each [employer(A) employee(B) employment(C)] 32. I've given the [explain(A) excuse(B) reason(C)] 33 for

leaving each position. I've given the names of three [applications(A) references(B) addresses(C)] 34.

I've described all my [skills(A) works(B) job(C)] 35, including languages I [know(A) can(B) how(C)] 36 speak. I've

[correct(A) listed(B) checked(C)] 37 the application to make sure it is complete.

F LISTENING ASSESSMENT: A Job Interview

Read and listen to the questions. Then listen to the job interview and answer the questions.

38. Where is the job interview probably taking place?
- (A) At a supermarket.
- (B) In a restaurant.
- (C) At a school.
- (D) In a department store.

39. When CAN'T the job applicant work?
- (A) Mornings
- (B) Afternoons.
- (C) Evenings.
- (D) Weekends.

40. How often are the employees paid?
- (A) Once a year.
- (B) Once a month.
- (C) Once a week.
- (D) Once a day.

. . . .

27 (A)(B)(C)(D)   31 (A)(B)(C)(D)   35 (A)(B)(C)(D)   39 (A)(B)(C)(D)

28 (A)(B)(C)(D)   32 (A)(B)(C)(D)   36 (A)(B)(C)(D)   40 (A)(B)(C)(D)

29 (A)(B)(C)(D)   33 (A)(B)(C)(D)   37 (A)(B)(C)(D)

30 (A)(B)(C)(D)   34 (A)(B)(C)(D)   38 (A)(B)(C)(D)

Go to the next page ⟩

G WRITING ASSESSMENT: A Job Application Form

Complete the job application form. (Use any information you wish.)

PERSONAL INFORMATION

NAME _____ SOCIAL SECURITY NUMBER _____
        LAST   FIRST   MIDDLE

ADDRESS _____ TELEPHONE _____
        NUMBER   STREET   CITY   STATE   ZIP CODE

EDUCATION HISTORY

HIGH SCHOOL _____ DIPLOMA OR GED RECEIVED: ___ YES ___ NO DATE _____
          NAME   CITY   STATE

COLLEGE/VOCATIONAL SCHOOL

NAME	LOCATION	FIELD OF STUDY	DEGREE/CERTIFICATION	DATE

EMPLOYMENT HISTORY (List most recent first.)

Date	Name & Address of Employer	Position	Salary	Name of Supervisor	Reason for Leaving
From: To:					
Duties					
From: To:					
Duties					
From: To:					
Duties					

SKILLS

LIST ANY SPECIAL TRAINING OR SKILLS YOU HAVE

_____

_____

SIGNATURE _____ DATE _____

H SPEAKING ASSESSMENT

I can ask and answer these questions:

Ask Answer

☐ ☐ Do you know how to _____?

☐ ☐ Have you seen _title of movie_ ?

Ask Answer

☐ ☐ What have you already done today?

☐ ☐ What haven't you done yet?

STOP

A GIVING PERSONAL INFORMATION ABOUT SELF, FAMILY, & JOB HISTORY

Example:

How long have you _____ a mechanic?
- Ⓐ are
- Ⓑ were
- Ⓒ be
- ● been

1. Have you always _____ here in Miami?
   - Ⓐ live
   - Ⓑ lived
   - Ⓒ living
   - Ⓓ you lived

2. How long have you _____ how to fix computers?
   - Ⓐ know
   - Ⓑ knew
   - Ⓒ known
   - Ⓓ knows

3. I've been a taxi driver _____ three years.
   - Ⓐ for
   - Ⓑ since
   - Ⓒ during
   - Ⓓ with

4. My family has lived here _____ 2001.
   - Ⓐ until
   - Ⓑ since
   - Ⓒ before
   - Ⓓ for

5. I've known how to speak French _____ a child.
   - Ⓐ for I'm
   - Ⓑ for I was
   - Ⓒ since I'm
   - Ⓓ since I was

6. Have you been a carpenter _____ a long time?
   - Ⓐ for
   - Ⓑ when
   - Ⓒ ago
   - Ⓓ since

7. _____ worked in my current job since May. Before that, _____ worked at a supermarket.
   - Ⓐ I . . . I
   - Ⓑ I . . . I've
   - Ⓒ I've . . . I
   - Ⓓ I've . . . I've

B STATING SKILLS, QUALIFICATIONS, & PERSONAL QUALITIES

Example:

I _____ type, file, and use a computer.
- Ⓐ known how
- Ⓑ known how to
- Ⓒ know how
- ● know how to

8. I _____.
   - Ⓐ hard work
   - Ⓑ harder work
   - Ⓒ work hard
   - Ⓓ am hard work

9. I have a lot of _____.
   - Ⓐ experience
   - Ⓑ employment
   - Ⓒ qualification
   - Ⓓ job

10. I'm never late. I'm very _____.
    - Ⓐ on time
    - Ⓑ for work
    - Ⓒ out of time
    - Ⓓ punctual

1 Ⓐ Ⓑ Ⓒ Ⓓ   4 Ⓐ Ⓑ Ⓒ Ⓓ   7 Ⓐ Ⓑ Ⓒ Ⓓ   9 Ⓐ Ⓑ Ⓒ Ⓓ

2 Ⓐ Ⓑ Ⓒ Ⓓ   5 Ⓐ Ⓑ Ⓒ Ⓓ   8 Ⓐ Ⓑ Ⓒ Ⓓ   10 Ⓐ Ⓑ Ⓒ Ⓓ

3 Ⓐ Ⓑ Ⓒ Ⓓ   6 Ⓐ Ⓑ Ⓒ Ⓓ

Go to the next page

Example:

_____ you working now?
- Ⓐ Will
- ● Are
- Ⓒ Have
- Ⓓ Do

11. Yes, I _____.
- Ⓐ do
- Ⓑ can
- Ⓒ am
- Ⓓ will

12. Where _____ you work now?
- Ⓐ have
- Ⓑ is
- Ⓒ did
- Ⓓ do

13. _____ at Tops Office Supplies.
- Ⓐ I work
- Ⓑ I worked
- Ⓒ I've worked
- Ⓓ I'll work

14. How long _____ there?
- Ⓐ do you work
- Ⓑ have you worked
- Ⓒ did you work
- Ⓓ does your work

15. _____ there since January.
- Ⓐ I work
- Ⓑ I worked
- Ⓒ I've worked
- Ⓓ I'll work

16. Where _____ before that?
- Ⓐ did you work
- Ⓑ have worked
- Ⓒ do you work
- Ⓓ you work

17. _____ at Shay's Supermarket.
- Ⓐ I work
- Ⓑ I'll work
- Ⓒ I've worked
- Ⓓ I worked

18. How long _____ there?
- Ⓐ you work
- Ⓑ do you work
- Ⓒ did you work
- Ⓓ have you worked

19. _____ two years.
- Ⓐ From
- Ⓑ For
- Ⓒ During
- Ⓓ Since

11 Ⓐ Ⓑ Ⓒ Ⓓ   14 Ⓐ Ⓑ Ⓒ Ⓓ   16 Ⓐ Ⓑ Ⓒ Ⓓ   18 Ⓐ Ⓑ Ⓒ Ⓓ
12 Ⓐ Ⓑ Ⓒ Ⓓ   15 Ⓐ Ⓑ Ⓒ Ⓓ   17 Ⓐ Ⓑ Ⓒ Ⓓ   19 Ⓐ Ⓑ Ⓒ Ⓓ
13 Ⓐ Ⓑ Ⓒ Ⓓ

Go to the next page ⟹

D **GRAMMAR IN CONTEXT: Clarifying to Ask for Meaning**

Example:
How long have you _____ unemployed?
- Ⓐ be
- ● been
- Ⓒ are
- Ⓓ was

20. I'm sorry. _____ does "unemployed" mean?
- Ⓐ Who
- Ⓑ What
- Ⓒ How
- Ⓓ Why

21. How long _____ out of work?
- Ⓐ you are
- Ⓑ you were
- Ⓒ have you been
- Ⓓ you have been

22. _____ two months.
- Ⓐ For
- Ⓑ Since
- Ⓒ With
- Ⓓ From

23. _____ you naturalized?
- Ⓐ Has
- Ⓑ Did
- Ⓒ Do
- Ⓓ Are

24. I'm sorry. What does that _____?
- Ⓐ say
- Ⓑ word
- Ⓒ mean
- Ⓓ understand

25. _____ you become a citizen yet?
- Ⓐ Do
- Ⓑ Are
- Ⓒ Has
- Ⓓ Have

26. Yes. _____ a citizen since 2003.
- Ⓐ I was
- Ⓑ I've been
- Ⓒ I'm not
- Ⓓ I have

27. _____ you ever been incarcerated?
- Ⓐ Have
- Ⓑ Did
- Ⓒ Were
- Ⓓ Was

28. I'm sorry. I don't _____ what that means.
- Ⓐ ask
- Ⓑ repeat
- Ⓒ understand
- Ⓓ sorry

Have you ever been in jail?

No, I haven't.

20 Ⓐ Ⓑ Ⓒ Ⓓ   23 Ⓐ Ⓑ Ⓒ Ⓓ   25 Ⓐ Ⓑ Ⓒ Ⓓ   27 Ⓐ Ⓑ Ⓒ Ⓓ
21 Ⓐ Ⓑ Ⓒ Ⓓ   24 Ⓐ Ⓑ Ⓒ Ⓓ   26 Ⓐ Ⓑ Ⓒ Ⓓ   28 Ⓐ Ⓑ Ⓒ Ⓓ
22 Ⓐ Ⓑ Ⓒ Ⓓ

Look at the job advertisements. Then do Numbers 29 through 32.

SaveMart is now hiring!

- Full Time, Part Time, & Sunday Only Positions
- Flexible Hours & Schedules
- Excellent Salary & Benefits
- Store Employee Discount

Positions now available:

Sales • Cashiers • Security

Ask for an application at the Service Desk.

★ **Join the** ★
Burger World Team!

- FREE MEALS
- FREE UNIFORMS
- PROMOTION OPPORTUNITIES
- REGULAR WAGE INCREASES
- ACADEMIC SCHOLARSHIPS

Counter, Crew, & Manager positions available

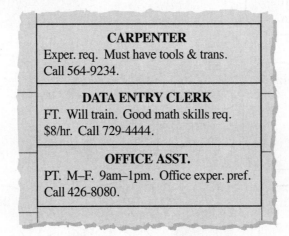

CARPENTER
Exper. req. Must have tools & trans. Call 564-9234.

DATA ENTRY CLERK
FT. Will train. Good math skills req. $8/hr. Call 729-4444.

OFFICE ASST.
PT. M–F. 9am–1pm. Office exper. pref. Call 426-8080.

29. Which job advertisement isn't in the newspaper?
    Ⓐ The ad for a carpenter.
    Ⓑ The ad for cashiers.
    Ⓒ The ad for an office assistant.
    Ⓓ The ad for a data entry clerk.

30. Which ad gives the best information about the salary?
    Ⓐ The ad for a salesperson.
    Ⓑ The ad for an office assistant.
    Ⓒ The ad for a carpenter.
    Ⓓ The ad for a data entry clerk.

31. Which statement about the office assistant position is NOT true?
    Ⓐ The position is part-time.
    Ⓑ The person will work 5 days a week.
    Ⓒ Experience is required.
    Ⓓ The person will work 20 hours a week.

32. Brenda already works full-time Monday through Friday. She wants to earn more money on weekends. Which job should she apply for?
    Ⓐ A job at SaveMart.
    Ⓑ A job at Burger World.
    Ⓒ The data entry clerk position.
    Ⓓ The office assistant position.

F GRAMMAR IN CONTEXT: Small Talk

Example:
_____ been?
- Ⓐ Are you
- Ⓑ How
- ● How have you
- Ⓓ How you have

33. _____ fine, thanks.
- Ⓐ I've been
- Ⓑ You've been
- Ⓒ You're
- Ⓓ I

34. How long _____ your daughter lived in Portland?
- Ⓐ is
- Ⓑ has
- Ⓒ was
- Ⓓ did

35. She's lived there _____ two years.
- Ⓐ since
- Ⓑ during
- Ⓒ in
- Ⓓ for

36. How long _____ your wife?
- Ⓐ you know
- Ⓓ you knew
- Ⓒ has
- Ⓓ have you known

37. I've known her since _____ in high school.
- Ⓐ we were
- Ⓑ we are
- Ⓒ we're
- Ⓓ she's

G LISTENING ASSESSMENT: Responding to a Job Ad; Abbreviations

Read and listen to the questions. Then listen to the conversation and answer the questions.

38. Which abbreviation describes the hours for this position?
- Ⓐ PT
- Ⓑ FT
- Ⓒ Flexible hrs.
- Ⓓ 8 hrs./wk.

39. Which statement describes the experience this job requires?
- Ⓐ Excel. benefits
- Ⓑ Typing skills pref.
- Ⓒ Office exper. req.
- Ⓓ Office exper. pref.

40. Which sentence is probably in the ad for this job?
- Ⓐ No calls.
- Ⓑ Apply in person.
- Ⓒ Call Pat at 421-2000.
- Ⓓ Ask for Pat at the service counter.

· ·

33 Ⓐ Ⓑ Ⓒ Ⓓ   35 Ⓐ Ⓑ Ⓒ Ⓓ   37 Ⓐ Ⓑ Ⓒ Ⓓ   39 Ⓐ Ⓑ Ⓒ Ⓓ

34 Ⓐ Ⓑ Ⓒ Ⓓ   36 Ⓐ Ⓑ Ⓒ Ⓓ   38 Ⓐ Ⓑ Ⓒ Ⓓ   40 Ⓐ Ⓑ Ⓒ Ⓓ

Write a resume. List your work experience, your education history, and your skills (languages you speak, computer skills, machines you can operate, licenses you have).

(Name)

(Address)

(Phone Number or E-mail)

WORK EXPERIENCE (LIST MOST RECENT FIRST)

Dates | Position, Place of Employment

City, State

Description of job duties

Dates | Position, Place of Employment

City, State

Description of job duties

Dates | Position, Place of Employment

City, State

Description of job duties

EDUCATION HISTORY

Dates | Degree or certificate

School, City, State

Dates | Degree or certificate

School, City, State

SKILLS

I **SPEAKING ASSESSMENT**

I can ask and answer these questions:

Ask	Answer		Ask	Answer	
☐	☐	Where do you live now?	☐	☐	Who is your best friend?
☐	☐	How long have you lived there?	☐	☐	How long have you known her/him?
☐	☐	Where did you live before that?	☐	☐	Who is the leader of your country?
☐	☐	How long did you live there?	☐	☐	How long has she/he been the leader?

STOP

A RENTING AN APARTMENT

Example:

How much is the _____?
- ● rent
- Ⓑ landlord
- Ⓒ utilities
- Ⓓ tenant

1. A rental agreement is _____.
   - Ⓐ a landlord
   - Ⓑ a lease
   - Ⓒ a utility
   - Ⓓ rent

2. Are pets _____ in the building?
   - Ⓐ permitted
   - Ⓑ permission
   - Ⓒ may I
   - Ⓓ rules

3. _____ utilities included in the rent?
   - Ⓐ Do
   - Ⓑ Does
   - Ⓒ Are
   - Ⓓ Is

4. What are the _____ of the building?
   - Ⓐ don't
   - Ⓑ allowed
   - Ⓒ permitted
   - Ⓓ rules

5. Does the rent _____ a parking space?
   - Ⓐ include
   - Ⓑ allowed
   - Ⓒ have
   - Ⓓ garage

6. Throw trash in the _____.
   - Ⓐ hallway
   - Ⓑ dumpster
   - Ⓒ recycling bin
   - Ⓓ garbage disposal

7. If something is broken, fill out a _____ request form.
   - Ⓐ pest control
   - Ⓑ problem
   - Ⓒ maintenance
   - Ⓓ building

8. It is prohibited to hang laundry on the _____.
   - Ⓐ entrance
   - Ⓑ apartment
   - Ⓒ balcony
   - Ⓓ place

9. Make sure you understand a lease before you _____ it.
   - Ⓐ deposit
   - Ⓑ write
   - Ⓒ rent
   - Ⓓ sign

1 Ⓐ Ⓑ Ⓒ Ⓓ   4 Ⓐ Ⓑ Ⓒ Ⓓ   7 Ⓐ Ⓑ Ⓒ Ⓓ

2 Ⓐ Ⓑ Ⓒ Ⓓ   5 Ⓐ Ⓑ Ⓒ Ⓓ   8 Ⓐ Ⓑ Ⓒ Ⓓ

3 Ⓐ Ⓑ Ⓒ Ⓓ   6 Ⓐ Ⓑ Ⓒ Ⓓ   9 Ⓐ Ⓑ Ⓒ Ⓓ

Go to the next page ⟶   **25** ●

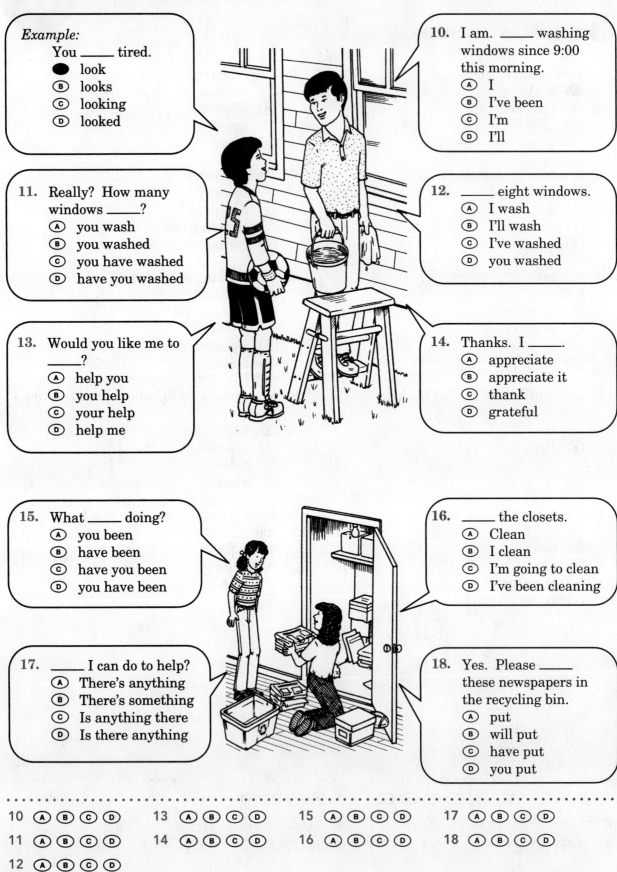

Example:
You _____ tired.
- ● look
- Ⓑ looks
- Ⓒ looking
- Ⓓ looked

10. I am. _____ washing windows since 9:00 this morning.
- Ⓐ I
- Ⓑ I've been
- Ⓒ I'm
- Ⓓ I'll

11. Really? How many windows _____?
- Ⓐ you wash
- Ⓑ you washed
- Ⓒ you have washed
- Ⓓ have you washed

12. _____ eight windows.
- Ⓐ I wash
- Ⓑ I'll wash
- Ⓒ I've washed
- Ⓓ you washed

13. Would you like me to _____?
- Ⓐ help you
- Ⓑ you help
- Ⓒ your help
- Ⓓ help me

14. Thanks. I _____.
- Ⓐ appreciate
- Ⓑ appreciate it
- Ⓒ thank
- Ⓓ grateful

15. What _____ doing?
- Ⓐ you been
- Ⓑ have been
- Ⓒ have you been
- Ⓓ you have been

16. _____ the closets.
- Ⓐ Clean
- Ⓑ I clean
- Ⓒ I'm going to clean
- Ⓓ I've been cleaning

17. _____ I can do to help?
- Ⓐ There's anything
- Ⓑ There's something
- Ⓒ Is anything there
- Ⓓ Is there anything

18. Yes. Please _____ these newspapers in the recycling bin.
- Ⓐ put
- Ⓑ will put
- Ⓒ have put
- Ⓓ you put

10 Ⓐ Ⓑ Ⓒ Ⓓ   13 Ⓐ Ⓑ Ⓒ Ⓓ   15 Ⓐ Ⓑ Ⓒ Ⓓ   17 Ⓐ Ⓑ Ⓒ Ⓓ

11 Ⓐ Ⓑ Ⓒ Ⓓ   14 Ⓐ Ⓑ Ⓒ Ⓓ   16 Ⓐ Ⓑ Ⓒ Ⓓ   18 Ⓐ Ⓑ Ⓒ Ⓓ

12 Ⓐ Ⓑ Ⓒ Ⓓ

Go to the next page ⇨

Name _____   Date _____

Look at the utility bill. Then do Numbers 19 through 22.

California Power and Light
P.O. Box 3566
Los Angeles, CA 90016
Web address: www.cpl.com

Customer assistance line
1-800-555-7600
To report a power outage
1-800-555-3000

Account Number **235-12-55-78304**
Hector Nieves
15 Park Drive
Los Angeles, CA 90020

Billing Date: 11/15/18
Payment Due: 12/10/18
Next Meter Read Date: 12/14/18

Billing Summary

Amount of Previous Statement 10/15/18	$ 89.91
Payment Received— 11/09/18 Thank You	89.91
Balance Before Current Charges	0.00
Current Charges	96.45
Your Total Balance Due	$ 96.45

Your current energy usage

Meter Number	From	To	Usage
AB910731	10/14/18	11/14/18	
	51291	51905	614 kilowatt hours

Reminder — a 9% late payment will be added to the total unpaid balance of your account if a full payment is not received by the due date on this bill.

Please write your account number on your check.

19. This is _____.
- Ⓐ a telephone bill
- Ⓑ an electric bill
- Ⓒ a gas bill
- Ⓓ a cable TV bill

20. Mr. Nieves has to pay this bill on or before _____.
- Ⓐ November 14
- Ⓑ November 15
- Ⓒ December 10
- Ⓓ December 14

21. The total amount due now is _____.
- Ⓐ 614 kilowatt hours
- Ⓑ $0.00
- Ⓒ $89.91
- Ⓓ $96.45

22. When Mr. Nieves pays this bill, he should write the number _____ on the check.
- Ⓐ 235-12-55-78304
- Ⓑ 1-800-555-7600
- Ⓒ 1-800-555-3000
- Ⓓ AB910731

19 Ⓐ Ⓑ Ⓒ Ⓓ   20 Ⓐ Ⓑ Ⓒ Ⓓ   21 Ⓐ Ⓑ Ⓒ Ⓓ   22 Ⓐ Ⓑ Ⓒ Ⓓ

Go to the next page ⟩

Look at the yellow pages listings. Then do Numbers 23 through 26.

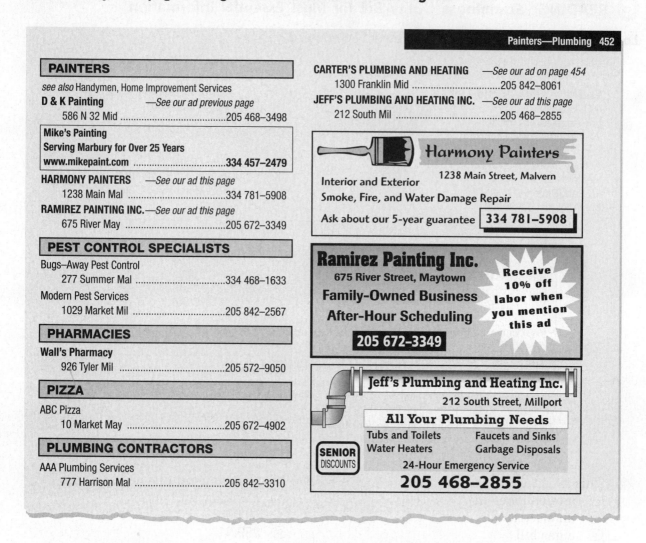

Painters—Plumbing 452

PAINTERS

see also Handymen, Home Improvement Services

D & K Painting *—See our ad previous page*
586 N 32 Mid 205 468–3498

Mike's Painting
Serving Marbury for Over 25 Years
www.mikepaint.com **334 457–2479**

HARMONY PAINTERS *—See our ad this page*
1238 Main Mal 334 781–5908

RAMIREZ PAINTING INC. *—See our ad this page*
675 River May 205 672–3349

PEST CONTROL SPECIALISTS

Bugs–Away Pest Control
277 Summer Mal 334 468–1633

Modern Pest Services
1029 Market Mil 205 842–2567

PHARMACIES

Wall's Pharmacy
926 Tyler Mil 205 572–9050

PIZZA

ABC Pizza
10 Market May 205 672–4902

PLUMBING CONTRACTORS

AAA Plumbing Services
777 Harrison Mal 205 842–3310

CARTER'S PLUMBING AND HEATING *—See our ad on page 454*
1300 Franklin Mid 205 842–8061

JEFF'S PLUMBING AND HEATING INC. *—See our ad this page*
212 South Mil 205 468–2855

Harmony Painters
1238 Main Street, Malvern
Interior and Exterior
Smoke, Fire, and Water Damage Repair
Ask about our 5-year guarantee | **334 781–5908**

Ramirez Painting Inc.
675 River Street, Maytown
Family-Owned Business
After-Hour Scheduling
205 672–3349
Receive 10% off labor when you mention this ad

Jeff's Plumbing and Heating Inc.
212 South Street, Millport
All Your Plumbing Needs
Tubs and Toilets   Faucets and Sinks
Water Heaters   Garbage Disposals
SENIOR DISCOUNTS
24-Hour Emergency Service
205 468–2855

---

23. You're looking for a painting company in Midfield. You should call ____.
Ⓐ 334 457-2479
Ⓑ 334 781-5908
Ⓒ 205 468-3498
Ⓓ 205 672-3349

24. There are roaches in your kitchen. You live in Malvern. You should call ____.
Ⓐ 334 457-2479
Ⓑ 334 468-1633
Ⓒ 205 842-2567
Ⓓ 205 572-9050

25. It's midnight. A pipe in your bathroom just broke. You should call ____.
Ⓐ 205 468-2855
Ⓑ 205 842-3310
Ⓒ 205 842-8061
Ⓓ 911

26. There isn't an ad for ____ on this page.
Ⓐ Harmony Painters
Ⓑ Jeff's Plumbing and Heating
Ⓒ Ramirez Painting
Ⓓ D & K Painting

Name _____   Date _____

E CLOZE READING: Housing Maintenance & Repairs

Choose the correct answers to complete the notice to tenants in an apartment building.

To: All Tenants
From: Your Building | Maintenance (A) | Mandatory (B) | Manager ● |

Please remember to follow these | reports (A) | rules (B) | requests (C) | [27] of the building:

Throw all trash in the | recycling bin (A) | dumpster (B) | hallway (C) | [28].

Put metal cans and | garbage (A) | landfill (B) | glass (C) | [29] in the recycling bins.

Don't forget: Recycling in our city is | mandatory (A) | waste (B) | routine (C) | [30].

Always turn on the water when you use the garbage | storage (A) | disposal (B) | bin (C) | [31].

Report any broken | pest (A) | kitchen (B) | smoke (C) | [32] detectors immediately.

Also report any other fire | safety (A) | hazards (B) | service (C) | [33].

Call the | rental (A) | storage (B) | common (C) | [34] office if you need the pest | collection (A) | control (B) | preparation (C) | [35] company.

Please do not call us with routine | maintenance (A) | emergency (B) | request (C) | [36] problems.

Fill out a maintenance request | program (A) | law (B) | form (C) | [37].

F LISTENING ASSESSMENT: Renting an Apartment

Read and listen to the questions. Then listen to the conversation and answer the questions.

38. Which pets are NOT allowed in the building?
- (A) Birds.
- (B) Small dogs.
- (C) Cats.
- (D) Large dogs.

39. Which utility is included in the rent?
- (A) Electricity.
- (B) Heat.
- (C) Cable TV.
- (D) Telephone.

40. Where can tenants park a second car?
- (A) In the parking lot.
- (B) In the garage.
- (C) In the rental office.
- (D) In the visitor parking spaces.

27 (A) (B) (C) (D)   31 (A) (B) (C) (D)   35 (A) (B) (C) (D)   39 (A) (B) (C) (D)

28 (A) (B) (C) (D)   32 (A) (B) (C) (D)   36 (A) (B) (C) (D)   40 (A) (B) (C) (D)

29 (A) (B) (C) (D)   33 (A) (B) (C) (D)   37 (A) (B) (C) (D)

30 (A) (B) (C) (D)   34 (A) (B) (C) (D)   38 (A) (B) (C) (D)   Go to the next page ⟩

Withdraw $200.00 from your savings account. Your account number is 83219745.

Deposit your paycheck for $575.25 in your account and get $100.00 in cash. Your account number is 42439182.

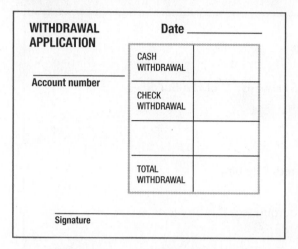

WITHDRAWAL APPLICATION	Date _____
Account number _____	CASH WITHDRAWAL
	CHECK WITHDRAWAL
	TOTAL WITHDRAWAL
Signature _____	

DEPOSIT SLIP	Date _____
Account number _____	CURRENCY
	COIN
Name _____	CHECKS
Sign here ONLY if cash received from deposit	LESS CASH
	TOTAL

Fill out the check to pay this bill.

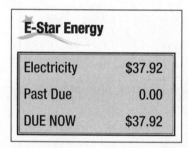

E-Star Energy

Electricity	$37.92
Past Due	0.00
DUE NOW	$37.92

	1024
	_____
Pay to the order of _____	$ _____
_____ Dollars	
For _____	_____
057009345 200042534 1024	

Now record this check in the check register and calculate the new balance.

Number	Date	Description	Amount of Debit (−)	Amount of Credit (+)	Balance
1022	1/14	Metrovision Cable TV	49.50		1,461.50
1023	1/16	Telecom	32.51		1,428.99

I can ask and answer these questions:

Ask Answer

☐ ☐ What street do you live on?

☐ ☐ How long have you been living on that street?

☐ ☐ Where else have you lived?

Ask Answer

☐ ☐ How long have you been studying English?

☐ ☐ Have you ever had a maintenance or repair problem where you live? What happened?

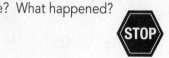

A REQUESTS AT WORK

Example:

Thank you _____ copying the report.
- (A) with
- (B) at
- (C) the
- (●) for

1. _____ clean the tables?
   - (A) Please you would
   - (B) Would please you
   - (C) Would you please
   - (D) Please would

2. Could I possibly _____ your pen?
   - (A) lend
   - (B) borrow
   - (C) lend me
   - (D) borrow you

3. Would you please _____ your calculator?
   - (A) borrow
   - (B) borrow me
   - (C) lend
   - (D) lend me

4. _____ happy to do it.
   - (A) I
   - (B) I be
   - (C) I'll be
   - (D) You

5. Thank you for _____ the chairs.
   - (A) setting up
   - (B) sets up
   - (C) set up
   - (D) you set up

6. _____ take the day off tomorrow?
   - (A) I'm possibly
   - (B) Could I possibly
   - (C) I could possibly
   - (D) Could possibly

7. Would you _____ help me with my presentation?
   - (A) possible
   - (B) can
   - (C) are able to
   - (D) be able to

8. I _____ take my son to a doctor's appointment tomorrow.
   - (A) have
   - (B) have to
   - (C) going
   - (D) going to

9. I'm asking for _____ tomorrow because my husband will be in the hospital.
   - (A) the day off
   - (B) the off day
   - (C) day off
   - (D) off day

....

1 (A) (B) (C) (D)   4 (A) (B) (C) (D)   7 (A) (B) (C) (D)

2 (A) (B) (C) (D)   5 (A) (B) (C) (D)   8 (A) (B) (C) (D)

3 (A) (B) (C) (D)   6 (A) (B) (C) (D)   9 (A) (B) (C) (D)

Go to the next page ➔ **31** ●

Example:

_____ set up the tables and chairs?
- Ⓐ Please
- Ⓑ You please
- ⬤ Would you please
- Ⓓ You would please

10. _____ be happy to.
- Ⓐ I
- Ⓑ I'll
- Ⓒ You
- Ⓓ You'll

11. Could I possibly _____ a screwdriver?
- Ⓐ borrow
- Ⓑ borrow you
- Ⓒ lend
- Ⓓ lend me

12. _____ Here you are.
- Ⓐ No.
- Ⓑ I'll be happy to.
- Ⓒ You'll be happy to.
- Ⓓ Sure.

13. Thank you _____ your cell phone.
- Ⓐ for borrowing
- Ⓑ for lending you
- Ⓒ for lending me
- Ⓓ please lend me

14. _____ welcome.
- Ⓐ You
- Ⓑ Your
- Ⓒ You're
- Ⓓ I'm

15. _____ was your weekend?
- Ⓐ Who
- Ⓑ What
- Ⓒ Where
- Ⓓ How

16. _____ was great.
- Ⓐ I
- Ⓑ It
- Ⓒ You
- Ⓓ We

17. What _____?
- Ⓐ you do
- Ⓑ did you
- Ⓒ you did
- Ⓓ did you do

18. We _____ to the beach.
- Ⓐ went
- Ⓑ go
- Ⓒ going
- Ⓓ gone

- -

10 Ⓐ Ⓑ Ⓒ Ⓓ   13 Ⓐ Ⓑ Ⓒ Ⓓ   15 Ⓐ Ⓑ Ⓒ Ⓓ   17 Ⓐ Ⓑ Ⓒ Ⓓ

11 Ⓐ Ⓑ Ⓒ Ⓓ   14 Ⓐ Ⓑ Ⓒ Ⓓ   16 Ⓐ Ⓑ Ⓒ Ⓓ   18 Ⓐ Ⓑ Ⓒ Ⓓ

12 Ⓐ Ⓑ Ⓒ Ⓓ

Go to the next page ▷

C READING: Workplace Notes & Messages

Look at the notes and messages. Then do Numbers 19 through 22.

BizNet

Mr. Lu,

    I'm sorry I was late this morning. My children's school bus didn't come this morning so I had to drive them to school. I'm writing my monthly report and will give it to you by the end of the day.

                Thanks,
                Gary

From the desk of
Wanda Torres

Alice,

    Thank you for buying the pizza and soda for yesterday's office party. Everything was great, and all the employees enjoyed themselves. Please give me your receipts as soon as you can and I'll reimburse you.

                Wanda

From:	Dawn_Kendall@BizNet.com
To:	Berta_Molina@BizNet.com
Subject:	New employee

Berta,
Our new office assistant, Luis Rodriguez, will begin work next Monday. Unfortunately, I won't be here that day because I have some meetings out of town. Could you please show Luis around the office and introduce him to all the employees? Also, please show him how to use the telephone system and bring him to the personnel office so he can get the new employee manual and fill out a W-4 form. Luis can spend the rest of the day reading last year's company report. I'll meet with him on Tuesday morning and talk with him about his job responsibilities.
Thanks very much,
Dawn

19. Next Monday, Luis Rodriguez WON'T _____.
- Ⓐ fill out a W-4 form
- Ⓑ meet his co-workers
- Ⓒ meet with Dawn Kendall
- Ⓓ begin work at the company

20. An employee is apologizing for something in _____ of these notes and messages.
- Ⓐ three
- Ⓑ two
- Ⓒ one
- Ⓓ none

21. In the note from Wanda to Alice, *reimburse* means _____.
- Ⓐ Alice will give Wanda money
- Ⓑ Wanda will give Alice money
- Ⓒ Alice's salary will be higher
- Ⓓ Wanda will buy the pizza and soda next time

22. We can infer from these notes and messages that _____.
- Ⓐ Alice is Wanda's supervisor
- Ⓑ Luis is Berta's new supervisor
- Ⓒ Luis is Dawn's new supervisor
- Ⓓ Mr. Lu is Gary's supervisor

19 Ⓐ Ⓑ Ⓒ Ⓓ   20 Ⓐ Ⓑ Ⓒ Ⓓ   21 Ⓐ Ⓑ Ⓒ Ⓓ   22 Ⓐ Ⓑ Ⓒ Ⓓ

Go to the next page ⟶

Look at the paycheck and pay stub. Then do Numbers 23 through 28.

TECHNOFILE CORPORATION			HADDAD F.		EMP. NO. 46803
PAY PERIOD					PAY DATE:
04/30/19 – 05/06/19					05/11/19

EARNINGS	RATE	HOURS	THIS PERIOD	YEAR TO DATE
REGULAR	16.00	35	560.00	7,280.00
OVERTIME	24.00	3	72.00	2,232.00
HOLIDAY	32.00	0	0.00	672.00
GROSS PAY			632.00	10,184.00

	THIS PERIOD	YEAR TO DATE	GROSS PAY	632.00
FED TAX	94.80	1,527.60	TAXES	170.64
FICA/MEDICARE	44.24	712.88	OTHER DEDUCTIONS	40.25
STATE TAX	31.60	509.20		
HEALTH	40.25	523.25		
			NET PAY	421.11

TF TECHNOFILE CORPORATION

Check No. | 2689412

Date Issued | 05/11/19

Pay to   FAISAL HADDAD

FOUR HUNDRED TWENTY-ONE DOLLARS AND ELEVEN CENTS   ***$421.11

Anna Rosario

23. Faisal's regular pay is
_____.
- Ⓐ $16.00 an hour
- Ⓑ $24.00 an hour
- Ⓒ $32.00 an hour
- Ⓓ $35.00 an hour

24. He worked a total of _____ during this pay period.
- Ⓐ 16 hours
- Ⓑ 24 hours
- Ⓒ 35 hours
- Ⓓ 38 hours

25. A pay period at the Technofile Corporation is _____.
- Ⓐ a day
- Ⓑ a week
- Ⓒ a month
- Ⓓ a year

26. Faisal earned _____ during this pay period before taxes and other deductions.
- Ⓐ $72.00
- Ⓑ $560.00
- Ⓒ $632.00
- Ⓓ $10,184.00

27. The deduction for state taxes since the beginning of the year is _____.
- Ⓐ $31.60
- Ⓑ $94.80
- Ⓒ $170.64
- Ⓓ $509.20

28. The company deducted a total of _____ from Faisal's salary during this pay period.
- Ⓐ $40.25
- Ⓑ $170.64
- Ⓒ $210.89
- Ⓓ $421.11

23 Ⓐ Ⓑ Ⓒ Ⓓ   25 Ⓐ Ⓑ Ⓒ Ⓓ   27 Ⓐ Ⓑ Ⓒ Ⓓ

24 Ⓐ Ⓑ Ⓒ Ⓓ   26 Ⓐ Ⓑ Ⓒ Ⓓ   28 Ⓐ Ⓑ Ⓒ Ⓓ

Go to the next page ⟶

E CLOZE READING: Small Talk at Work

Choose the correct answers to complete the paragraph.

"Small talk" at work is important. The short conversations that people have with

its   their   our   co-workers show that they   be   was   are   29 friendly. There are many
Ⓐ   ●   Ⓒ   Ⓐ   Ⓑ   Ⓒ

good questions to begin small talk: "What   do   did   will   30 you do last weekend?" "What
                                            Ⓐ   Ⓑ   Ⓒ

are you   will   going   going to   31 do next weekend?" "Did you see the football game on TV
           Ⓐ   Ⓑ   Ⓒ

yesterday   tomorrow   next week   32?" Other safe topics are hobbies, movies, TV programs,
Ⓐ   Ⓑ   Ⓒ

and the   weather   weathers   whether   33. You can talk about the news, but avoid
           Ⓐ   Ⓑ   Ⓒ

to talk   talking   don't talk   34 about politics.   Sharing   Share   You Share   35 information
Ⓐ   Ⓑ   Ⓒ   Ⓐ   Ⓑ   Ⓒ

about your family can be a good topic for small talk, but co-workers won't like

hear   listen   hearing   36 about serious family problems. Listening is also an important part
Ⓐ   Ⓑ   Ⓒ

of small talk.   Listening   Listen   You listen   37 carefully to what your co-workers are saying, and
                  Ⓐ   Ⓑ   Ⓒ

ask questions to show you're interested.

F LISTENING ASSESSMENT: Two Co-Workers Talking at the Office

Read and listen to the questions. Then listen to the conversation and answer the questions.

38. Who just had a baby?
- Ⓐ Tonya.
- Ⓑ Leona.
- Ⓒ Ken's wife.
- Ⓓ Ken's sister.

39. What are Tonya and Barry thinking about doing?
- Ⓐ Buying a house.
- Ⓑ Getting an apartment outside the city.
- Ⓒ Moving to a new apartment in their building.
- Ⓓ Buying a new TV.

40. How did Ken go to Tampa?
- Ⓐ He went by bus.
- Ⓑ He probably went by airplane.
- Ⓒ He went by car.
- Ⓓ This information isn't in the conversation.

. . . .

29 Ⓐ Ⓑ Ⓒ Ⓓ   33 Ⓐ Ⓑ Ⓒ Ⓓ   37 Ⓐ Ⓑ Ⓒ Ⓓ

30 Ⓐ Ⓑ Ⓒ Ⓓ   34 Ⓐ Ⓑ Ⓒ Ⓓ   38 Ⓐ Ⓑ Ⓒ Ⓓ

31 Ⓐ Ⓑ Ⓒ Ⓓ   35 Ⓐ Ⓑ Ⓒ Ⓓ   39 Ⓐ Ⓑ Ⓒ Ⓓ

32 Ⓐ Ⓑ Ⓒ Ⓓ   36 Ⓐ Ⓑ Ⓒ Ⓓ   40 Ⓐ Ⓑ Ⓒ Ⓓ

Go to the next page ⟹

Complete the form with your own information or make up any information you wish.

Form W-4

Purpose. Complete Form W-4 so that your employer can withhold the correct federal income tax from your pay.

Head of household. You are the head of household if you pay more than 50% of the costs of keeping up a home for yourself and your dependents.

Personal Allowances Worksheet

A   Enter "1" for **yourself** if no one else can claim you as a dependent.. A _____

B   Enter "1" if
- You are single and have only one job; or
- You are married, have only one job, and your spouse does not work; or
- Your wages from a second job or your spouse's wages are $1,500 or less.

} .... B _____

C   Enter "1" for your **spouse**. -- C _____

D   Enter number of **dependents**.-- D _____

E   Enter "1" if you will file as **head of household** on your tax return.---------------------------------- E _____

F   Enter "1" if you have at least $1,500 of **child or dependent care expenses**.------------------------ F _____

G   **Child Tax Credit**
- If your total income is less than $58,000 ($86,000 if married), enter "2" for each child.
- If your total income is between $58,000 and $84,000 ($86,000 and $119,000 if married), enter "1" for each child. --- G _____

H   Add lines A through G and enter total here.-- ► H _____

Stop here and enter the number from line H on line 5 of Form W-4 below.

Form **W-4**   ## Employee's Withholding Allowance Certificate

1 Type or print your first name and middle initial.	Last name	**2** Your social security number
Home address (number and street or rural route)	**3** ☐ Single ☐ Married ☐ Married, but withhold at higher Single rate.	
City or town, state, and ZIP code	**4** If your last name is different from the one on your social security card, check here. You must call 1-800-772-1213 for a replacement card. ☐	

5 Total number of allowances you are claiming (from line **H** above)_____	**5**
6 Additional amount, if any, you want withheld from each paycheck _____	**6**

7 I claim exemption from withholding, and I meet **both** of the following conditions.
- Last year I had a right to a refund of **all** federal income tax withheld because I had **no** tax liability **and**
- This year I expect a refund of **all** federal income tax withheld because I expect to have **no** tax liability.
If you meet both conditions write "Exempt" here --- ► **7**

Under penalties of perjury, I declare that I have examined this certificate and to the best of my knowledge and belief, it is true, correct, and complete.

Employee's signature
(Form is not valid
unless you sign it.) ►   **Date** ►

I can ask and answer these questions:

Ask Answer
☐ ☐ What did you do last weekend?
☐ ☐ What are you going to do next weekend?

Ask Answer
☐ ☐ What do you enjoy doing in your free time?
☐ ☐ What do you avoid doing whenever you can?

STOP

A HEALTH & NUTRITION

Example:

I'd like to make _____.
- Ⓐ cancel
- Ⓑ reschedule
- ● an appointment
- Ⓓ a doctor's office

1. Can you _____ on Friday at 10:00?
   - Ⓐ convenient
   - Ⓑ convenient time
   - Ⓒ come in
   - Ⓓ would be fine

2. You should have a physical _____ every year.
   - Ⓐ history
   - Ⓑ examination
   - Ⓒ vaccination
   - Ⓓ prescription

3. I have to get a _____ shot.
   - Ⓐ dental
   - Ⓑ clinic
   - Ⓒ cholesterol
   - Ⓓ flu

4. Do you take any prescription _____?
   - Ⓐ drugs
   - Ⓑ operations
   - Ⓒ tests
   - Ⓓ diseases

5. The _____ on the food pyramid show the different food groups.
   - Ⓐ grains
   - Ⓑ products
   - Ⓒ steps
   - Ⓓ stripes

6. Dark green and orange vegetables contain more _____ than starchy vegetables.
   - Ⓐ juice
   - Ⓑ dairy products
   - Ⓒ nutrients
   - Ⓓ cholesterol

7. The oil from _____ is good for your heart.
   - Ⓐ fish
   - Ⓑ butter
   - Ⓒ margarine
   - Ⓓ ice cream

8. The grain group consists of foods made from wheat, rice, or _____.
   - Ⓐ vegetables
   - Ⓑ oils
   - Ⓒ corn
   - Ⓓ milk

9. I have a bad cough. I'm going to _____.
   - Ⓐ go to the emergency room
   - Ⓑ go to the clinic
   - Ⓒ call 911
   - Ⓓ get a vaccination

1 Ⓐ Ⓑ Ⓒ Ⓓ   4 Ⓐ Ⓑ Ⓒ Ⓓ   7 Ⓐ Ⓑ Ⓒ Ⓓ
2 Ⓐ Ⓑ Ⓒ Ⓓ   5 Ⓐ Ⓑ Ⓒ Ⓓ   8 Ⓐ Ⓑ Ⓒ Ⓓ
3 Ⓐ Ⓑ Ⓒ Ⓓ   6 Ⓐ Ⓑ Ⓒ Ⓓ   9 Ⓐ Ⓑ Ⓒ Ⓓ

Example:
How long _____ coughing like this?
- (A) are you
- (B) you are
- (C) you've been
- ● have you been

10. _____ a few days.
- (A) Since
- (B) From
- (C) With
- (D) For

11. How long have your legs _____ swollen?
- (A) are
- (B) being
- (C) been
- (D) be

12. _____ last Monday.
- (A) Since
- (B) During
- (C) For
- (D) Began

13. When _____ first see these bruises on your arm?
- (A) you did
- (B) did you
- (C) you have
- (D) have you

14. I don't know. _____ them for a while.
- (A) I'll have
- (B) I'm having
- (C) I had
- (D) I've had

15. _____ this area here feel tender?
- (A) Do
- (B) Does
- (C) Have
- (D) Has

16. Ouch! Yes. _____ felt tender since I fell down the stairs.
- (A) I
- (B) They have
- (C) It has
- (D) I was

17. You have a _____. I can take care of it today.
- (A) filling
- (B) tooth
- (C) gum
- (D) cavity

18. Can I have a silver _____?
- (A) filling
- (B) tooth
- (C) gum
- (D) cavity

Yes, you can.

Okay.

. . . .

10 (A) (B) (C) (D)   13 (A) (B) (C) (D)   15 (A) (B) (C) (D)   17 (A) (B) (C) (D)

11 (A) (B) (C) (D)   14 (A) (B) (C) (D)   16 (A) (B) (C) (D)   18 (A) (B) (C) (D)

12 (A) (B) (C) (D)

Go to the next page ⇒

C READING: Medical Appointment Cards

These people have medical appointments during the next few months. Read the appointment cards. Then do Numbers 19 through 22.

COMMUNITY MEDICAL CLINIC
4600 N. Federal Highway, Miami, FL 33137

Quan Vu

HAS AN APPOINTMENT ON

Mon.   Oct.   10th   at   11   (A.M.)
DAY   MONTH   DATE   P.M.

IF UNABLE TO KEEP THIS APPOINTMENT, PLEASE GIVE ONE DAY ADVANCE NOTICE.
TELEPHONE: (305) 576-7000

APPOINTMENT

FOR _____ _Gloria Salinas_ _____

ON ___ Thu.   Nov.   3 ___ AT __ 2:00 (A.M. P.M.)
         DAY   MONTH   DATE

GLENDALE HEALTH CENTER
501 North Glendale Avenue
Glendale, CA 91206
(818) 500-8762

IF UNABLE TO KEEP THIS APPOINTMENT, KINDLY GIVE 24 HOURS NOTICE.

M _____ **Ahmed Samra** _____

HAS AN APPOINTMENT ON

☐ MON   ☐ TUE   ☐ WED   ☐ THU   ☐ FRI   ☑ SAT

OCT   22   AT   3:15 (A.M. P.M.)
MONTH   DATE

✚ SUNNYSIDE HEALTH CENTER
9314 Cullen Blvd.   TEL (713) 732-5000
Houston, TX 77051

**PATIENTS WILL BE CHARGED FOR APPOINTMENTS
NOT CANCELED AT LEAST 24 HOURS IN ADVANCE.**

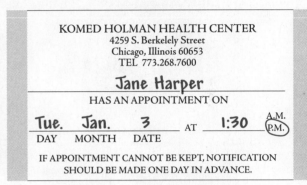

KOMED HOLMAN HEALTH CENTER
4259 S. Berkelely Street
Chicago, Illinois 60653
TEL 773.268.7600

Jane Harper

HAS AN APPOINTMENT ON

Tue.   Jan.   3   AT ___ 1:30 (A.M. P.M.)
DAY   MONTH   DATE

IF APPOINTMENT CANNOT BE KEPT, NOTIFICATION
SHOULD BE MADE ONE DAY IN ADVANCE.

19. Which day of the week is Gloria's appointment?
    Ⓐ Tuesday
    Ⓑ Thursday
    Ⓒ November
    Ⓓ the 3rd

20. Which patient has an appointment in the morning?
    Ⓐ Jane Harper
    Ⓑ Gloria Salinas
    Ⓒ Ahmed Samra
    Ⓓ Quan Vu

21. Which health center is definitely open during part of the weekend?
    Ⓐ Community Medical Clinic
    Ⓑ Glendale Health Center
    Ⓒ Sunnyside Health Center
    Ⓓ Komed Holman Health Center

22. Whose appointment is next year?
    Ⓐ Jane Harper
    Ⓑ Gloria Salinas
    Ⓒ Ahmed Samra
    Ⓓ Quan Vu

19 Ⓐ Ⓑ Ⓒ Ⓓ   20 Ⓐ Ⓑ Ⓒ Ⓓ   21 Ⓐ Ⓑ Ⓒ Ⓓ   22 Ⓐ Ⓑ Ⓒ Ⓓ

Go to the next page ⇨

Look at the illustrations. Choose the correct answer.

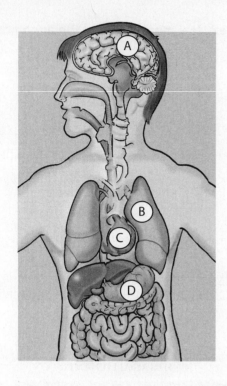

Example: stomach	(A) (B) (C) ●
23. brain	(A) (B) (C) (D)
24. heart	(A) (B) (C) (D)
25. lungs	(A) (B) (C) (D)

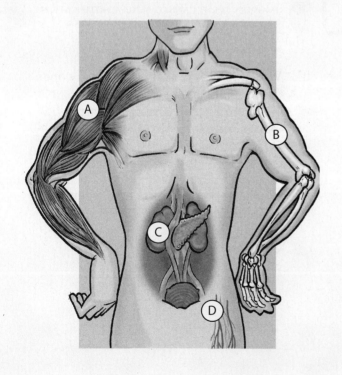

26. veins	(A) (B) (C) (D)
27. bones	(A) (B) (C) (D)
28. kidneys	(A) (B) (C) (D)
29. muscles	(A) (B) (C) (D)

23 (A) (B) (C) (D)   25 (A) (B) (C) (D)   27 (A) (B) (C) (D)   29 (A) (B) (C) (D)

24 (A) (B) (C) (D)   26 (A) (B) (C) (D)   28 (A) (B) (C) (D)

Go to the next page ⟩

E CLOZE READING: Public Health Information

Choose the correct answers to complete the newspaper article.

New Health Center Opens

WARNER—The new Downtown Health Center opened yesterday. The

examination clinic emergency offers health care to all city residents. It is a drop-in medical center,
  (A)   ●   (C)

so no service routine appointment 30 is necessary. For patients who don't understand English well,
     (A)   (B)   (C)

vaccination translation medication 31 is available in 15 different languages. Patients pay for medical
  (A)   (B)   (C)

care based on how much they earn since the clinic's fees are on a sliding scale range care 32. Patients
                    (A)   (B)   (C)

can have a physical guideline operation examination 33 every year, including a
         (A)   (B)   (C)

cholesterol tetanus skin 34 blood test and other screening tests. The clinic also provides flu shots and
  (A)   (B)   (C)

other prescriptions vaccinations schedules 35. It is across the street from Warner General Hospital,
     (A)   (B)   (C)

a full-service hospital with 500 beds and a 24-hour serious 911 emergency 36 room. Patients should
                        (A) (B)   (C)

go there or call an ambulance for health problems such as a cough a broken leg an earache 37.
                            (A)   (B)   (C)

Patients with routine medical problems should use the clinic.

F LISTENING ASSESSMENT: Calling about a Medical Appointment

Read and listen to the questions. Then listen to the conversation and answer the questions.

38. Why is Victoria calling the doctor's office?
- (A) To make a new appointment.
- (B) To cancel an appointment.
- (C) To reschedule an appointment.
- (D) To confirm an appointment.

39. When was she scheduled to come in?
- (A) Thu. Apr. 15 4:00
- (B) Tue. Apr. 20 11:00
- (C) Thu. Apr. 20 11:00
- (D) Tue. Apr. 13 10:00

40. When is her new appointment?
- (A) Thu. Apr. 15 4:00
- (B) Tue. Apr. 20 11:00
- (C) Thu. Apr. 20 11:00
- (D) Tue. Apr. 13 10:00

30 (A) (B) (C) (D)   33 (A) (B) (C) (D)   36 (A) (B) (C) (D)   39 (A) (B) (C) (D)

31 (A) (B) (C) (D)   34 (A) (B) (C) (D)   37 (A) (B) (C) (D)   40 (A) (B) (C) (D)

32 (A) (B) (C) (D)   35 (A) (B) (C) (D)   38 (A) (B) (C) (D)

Go to the next page ⟩

WRITING ASSESSMENT: A Medical History Form

Complete the form with your own information or make up any information you wish.

MEDICAL HISTORY

Name _____ Date of Birth _____

List the medications you are now taking. Include non-prescription drugs and vitamins.

_____

List any allergies you have to drugs, food, or other items. _____

_____

List any operations you have had, including the year. _____

_____

Please check if you have had any of the following health problems.

____ chicken pox	____ diabetes	____ depression
____ measles	____ tuberculosis	____ frequent earaches
____ mumps	____ cancer	____ severe headaches
____ asthma	____ AIDS	____ back problems
____ heart disease	____ kidney disease	____ frequent colds
____ high blood pressure	____ liver disease (hepatitis)	____ stomach problems
____ pneumonia	____ influenza	____ loss of appetite

FAMILY HISTORY

Please check if anyone in your family (parents, siblings, grandparents, children) has had any of the following illnesses.

____ asthma	____ diabetes	____ AIDS
____ heart disease	____ tuberculosis	____ kidney disease
____ high blood pressure	____ cancer	____ liver disease

RECORD OF IMMUNIZATIONS

Please check if you had any of the following vaccinations or tests, and fill in the year of the most recent ones.

	Year
____ measles	
____ mumps	
____ chicken pox	
____ tetanus	

	Year
____ tuberculosis test	
____ hepatitis B	
____ influenza	
____ pneumonia	

SPEAKING ASSESSMENT

I can ask and answer these questions:

Ask Answer

☐ ☐ How often do you have a physical examination at a doctor's office or a clinic?

☐ ☐ Where do you go for medical care?

Ask Answer

☐ ☐ What vegetables and fruit do you eat?

☐ ☐ What foods should you eat more of?

☐ ☐ What foods should you eat less of?

STOP

A   SHOPPING

Example:

I'm _____ a pair of pants.
- Ⓐ want
- Ⓑ need
- Ⓒ looking
- ● looking for

1. This dress is 20% off this week.
   We're having a special _____.
   - Ⓐ regular price
   - Ⓑ half-price
   - Ⓒ sale
   - Ⓓ reduced

2. You can try on these pants in the _____.
   - Ⓐ mall
   - Ⓑ cleaner's
   - Ⓒ pants room
   - Ⓓ dressing room

3. I like to buy things when they're _____.
   - Ⓐ discount
   - Ⓑ on sale
   - Ⓒ the sign on the rack
   - Ⓓ bargain

4. My jacket size is _____.
   - Ⓐ 20% off
   - Ⓑ half-price
   - Ⓒ large
   - Ⓓ reduced

5. I don't want to exchange it. I'd like _____, please.
   - Ⓐ the matter
   - Ⓑ a return
   - Ⓒ a receipt
   - Ⓓ a refund

6. All our shirts are 15 _____ off the regular price this week.
   - Ⓐ percent
   - Ⓑ price
   - Ⓒ reduced
   - Ⓓ half

7. You can use this coupon until the _____.
   - Ⓐ regular price
   - Ⓑ expiration date
   - Ⓒ newspaper ad
   - Ⓓ refund

8. These tee shirts are usually $16, but they're only $12 this week. They're _____.
   - Ⓐ 10% off
   - Ⓑ 20% off
   - Ⓒ 25% off
   - Ⓓ half-price

9. All our $60 men's jeans are $40 this week. They're _____ the regular price.
   - Ⓐ 1/3 off
   - Ⓑ 1/2 off
   - Ⓒ 20% off
   - Ⓓ 40% off

. . . .

1 Ⓐ Ⓑ Ⓒ Ⓓ   4 Ⓐ Ⓑ Ⓒ Ⓓ   7 Ⓐ Ⓑ Ⓒ Ⓓ

2 Ⓐ Ⓑ Ⓒ Ⓓ   5 Ⓐ Ⓑ Ⓒ Ⓓ   8 Ⓐ Ⓑ Ⓒ Ⓓ

3 Ⓐ Ⓑ Ⓒ Ⓓ   6 Ⓐ Ⓑ Ⓒ Ⓓ   9 Ⓐ Ⓑ Ⓒ Ⓓ

Go to the next page ⟩ **43**

Example:

I'd like to exchange ＿＿＿ jacket.
- ● this
- Ⓑ that
- Ⓒ these
- Ⓓ those

RETURN POLICY

10. What's the matter with ＿＿＿?
- Ⓐ you
- Ⓑ that
- Ⓒ this
- Ⓓ it

11. Three buttons ＿＿＿ missing.
- Ⓐ be
- Ⓑ is
- Ⓒ are
- Ⓓ will be

12. All right. Please get another jacket from the rack, ＿＿＿ here, and I'll be happy to help you.
- Ⓐ bring back
- Ⓑ bring it back
- Ⓒ bring back it
- Ⓓ it bring back

13. I'd like to return ＿＿＿ pants.
- Ⓐ this
- Ⓑ that
- Ⓒ these
- Ⓓ those

14. What's the matter with ＿＿＿?
- Ⓐ it
- Ⓑ you
- Ⓒ those
- Ⓓ them

15. The zipper ＿＿＿ broken.
- Ⓐ be
- Ⓑ is
- Ⓒ are
- Ⓓ did

16. ＿＿＿ your receipt?
- Ⓐ You have
- Ⓑ Do have
- Ⓒ Do you have
- Ⓓ You do have

17. Yes. ＿＿＿
- Ⓐ Here it is.
- Ⓑ Here I am.
- Ⓒ Here they are.
- Ⓓ It is.

18. ＿＿＿ exchange them?
- Ⓐ Do you like to
- Ⓑ You do like to
- Ⓒ You would like to
- Ⓓ Would you like to

19. No, thank you. ＿＿＿ a refund, please.
- Ⓐ I like
- Ⓑ I'd like
- Ⓒ I'll like
- Ⓓ You give

20. Okay. Here's our merchandise return form. Please ＿＿＿ and I'll give you a refund.
- Ⓐ fill
- Ⓑ fill out
- Ⓒ fill out it
- Ⓓ fill it out

. . . .

10 Ⓐ Ⓑ Ⓒ Ⓓ   13 Ⓐ Ⓑ Ⓒ Ⓓ   16 Ⓐ Ⓑ Ⓒ Ⓓ   19 Ⓐ Ⓑ Ⓒ Ⓓ

11 Ⓐ Ⓑ Ⓒ Ⓓ   14 Ⓐ Ⓑ Ⓒ Ⓓ   17 Ⓐ Ⓑ Ⓒ Ⓓ   20 Ⓐ Ⓑ Ⓒ Ⓓ

12 Ⓐ Ⓑ Ⓒ Ⓓ   15 Ⓐ Ⓑ Ⓒ Ⓓ   18 Ⓐ Ⓑ Ⓒ Ⓓ

Go to the next page ⇨

Name _____ Date _____

Look at the clothing store advertisement. Then do Numbers 21 through 24.

CARTER'S DEPARTMENT STORE

Biggest Sale of the Year!!!
Thursday thru Saturday, October 10-12

$19.99
50%–60% off
Men's dress shirts
Orig. $40-$50

Lana Lee tee shirts
Orig. $20
NOW 2/$25 OR $15 EACH

Speedway Running Shoes
Reg. $80
SALE $40

Warner Men's Jeans
Reg. $40
SALE $30

All Nina Sanders skirts
HALF PRICE
SALE $25

21. During the sale, Speedway Running Shoes are ____.
    Ⓐ 10% off
    Ⓑ 40% off
    Ⓒ $80.00
    Ⓓ half-price

22. Fatima is going to buy four tee shirts during the sale. How much is she going to spend?
    Ⓐ $50
    Ⓑ $60
    Ⓒ $70
    Ⓓ $80

23. The regular price of Nina Sanders skirts is ____.
    Ⓐ $25
    Ⓑ $50
    Ⓒ $75
    Ⓓ $100

24. The men's jeans are ____ during the sale.
    Ⓐ 10% off
    Ⓑ 20% off
    Ⓒ 25% off
    Ⓓ 30% off

21 Ⓐ Ⓑ Ⓒ Ⓓ   22 Ⓐ Ⓑ Ⓒ Ⓓ   23 Ⓐ Ⓑ Ⓒ Ⓓ   24 Ⓐ Ⓑ Ⓒ Ⓓ

Go to the next page

Look at the coupons for these food products. Then do Numbers 25 through 30.

25. You bought a loaf of Alan's bread
    with a coupon and paid $2.00. The
    original price was _____.
    - Ⓐ $1.50
    - Ⓑ $2.00
    - Ⓒ $2.50
    - Ⓓ $3.00

26. A box of Happy Heart cereal costs
    $3.00. With a coupon you pay _____
    for three boxes.
    - Ⓐ $5.00
    - Ⓑ $6.00
    - Ⓒ $7.50
    - Ⓓ $9.00

27. You can't use the coupon for _____
    after September 18, 2020.
    - Ⓐ Bob & Joe's Ice Cream
    - Ⓑ Maxima Coffee
    - Ⓒ Farmtown Yogurt
    - Ⓓ Pollyana Jam

28. Ramona bought one pint of Bob & Joe's Ice
    Cream. The regular price is $4.50. She paid
    _____.
    - Ⓐ $1.00
    - Ⓑ $3.50
    - Ⓒ $4.00
    - Ⓓ $4.50

29. A 6 oz. container of Farmtown Yogurt costs
    $1.00. With a coupon you pay a total of
    _____ when you buy ten.
    - Ⓐ $9.00
    - Ⓑ $9.50
    - Ⓒ $10.00
    - Ⓓ 90¢

30. You bought two cans of Maxima Coffee with
    a coupon and paid $9.00. The regular price
    of one can is _____.
    - Ⓐ $4.50
    - Ⓑ $5.00
    - Ⓒ $5.50
    - Ⓓ $6.00

25 Ⓐ Ⓑ Ⓒ Ⓓ   27 Ⓐ Ⓑ Ⓒ Ⓓ   29 Ⓐ Ⓑ Ⓒ Ⓓ

26 Ⓐ Ⓑ Ⓒ Ⓓ   28 Ⓐ Ⓑ Ⓒ Ⓓ   30 Ⓐ Ⓑ Ⓒ Ⓓ

Go to the next page ⇨

E CLOZE READING: A Store Return Policy

Choose the correct answers to complete the sign in a store's Customer Service Department.

Pratt's Department Store

Our Return Policy

- You may receipt refund **return** most items within 90 days of the date of purchase.
  (A)   (B)   ●

- We will back take back take them back [31] computers and printers only within 45 days
  (A)   (B)   (C)

  of the date of purchase.

- If you want to return CDs or DVDs, you must bring bring back bring them back [32]
  (A)   (B)   (C)

  within 30 days of the date of purchase, and they must be opened unopened on sale [33].
  (A)   (B)   (C)

- We cannot accept returns on items marked Final Sale Refund Credit [34].
  (A)   (B)   (C)

- To receive a refund, you must provide your return receipt purchase [35] for the item. If
  (A)   (B)   (C)

  you don't have it, you can buy accept exchange [36] the item for another one or you can
  (A)   (B)   (C)

  receive a gift card with a store credit for the amount of the purchase.

- You may return a defective item at any time, and we will repair break buy [37] it or give
  (A)   (B)   (C)

  you a new item.

F LISTENING ASSESSMENT: Returning Items to a Store

Read and listen to the questions. Then listen to the conversation and answer the questions.

38. How many items is the customer returning to the store?
- (A) One.
- (B) Two.
- (C) Three.
- (D) Four.

39. What's the matter with the blouse?
- (A) A button is missing.
- (B) Two buttons are missing.
- (C) A sleeve is stained.
- (D) The sleeves are stained.

40. Why can't the customer receive a refund?
- (A) The coat and the blouse are defective.
- (B) The customer wants to exchange the items.
- (C) The customer doesn't have a gift card.
- (D) The customer doesn't have the receipt.

· ·

31 (A) (B) (C) (D)   34 (A) (B) (C) (D)   37 (A) (B) (C) (D)   40 (A) (B) (C) (D)

32 (A) (B) (C) (D)   35 (A) (B) (C) (D)   38 (A) (B) (C) (D)

33 (A) (B) (C) (D)   36 (A) (B) (C) (D)   39 (A) (B) (C) (D)   **Go to the next page** ⟩

G WRITING ASSESSMENT: A Product Return Form

You are returning an item to a store in your community. Complete the form with your personal information, and make up information about the product you are returning.

PRODUCT RETURN FORM

1. CUSTOMER INFORMATION

Name _____

Address _____

City _____ State _____ Zip Code _____

Telephone: Home (_____) _____-_____   Work (_____) _____-_____

2. PRODUCT INFORMATION

Product being returned: _____

Store where purchased (name, city, state): _____

Purchase date: _____

Please describe problem with product: _____

_____

3. REFUND/EXCHANGE INFORMATION

Please check one:

_____ I request a refund. (Store receipt required.)

_____ I will exchange the product for another one of the same item.

_____ I request a store credit for the amount of the purchase.

_____ Other (Explain: _____)

Customer Signature: _____ Today's Date: _____

H SPEAKING ASSESSMENT

I can ask and answer these questions:

Ask Answer
☐ ☐ Where do you shop for clothing?
☐ ☐ What kind of clothing do you like to wear?

Ask Answer
☐ ☐ Have you ever bought something on sale?
☐ ☐ What did you buy, and where?

Ask Answer
☐ ☐ Have you ever returned an item to a store?
☐ ☐ What did you return, and where?

STOP

A WORKPLACE COMMUNICATION & CAREER ADVANCEMENT

Example:
Excuse me. Can you _____?
- Ⓐ I help
- Ⓑ my help
- ⬤ help me
- Ⓓ me help

1. Please _____ make a copy.
- Ⓐ how to
- Ⓑ show me how
- Ⓒ you show me how to
- Ⓓ show me how to

2. _____, add the water. Then, press the ON button.
- Ⓐ Sure
- Ⓑ First
- Ⓒ Finally
- Ⓓ And finally

3. I'm friendly at work. I _____ my co-workers.
- Ⓐ get
- Ⓑ get along
- Ⓒ get along with
- Ⓓ along with

4. I try to always have a positive _____ at work.
- Ⓐ compliment
- Ⓑ attitude
- Ⓒ feedback
- Ⓓ promotion

5. Appropriate clothes and good grooming are important parts of your _____ at work.
- Ⓐ appearance
- Ⓑ opportunity
- Ⓒ energy
- Ⓓ creativity

6. When a co-worker does something well, _____.
- Ⓐ apologize
- Ⓑ complain
- Ⓒ volunteer
- Ⓓ give a compliment

7. It's important to continue your _____ to learn new skills.
- Ⓐ promotion
- Ⓑ evaluation
- Ⓒ education
- Ⓓ presentation

8. If you want to move ahead at work, ask for more _____.
- Ⓐ skills
- Ⓑ responsibilities
- Ⓒ compliments
- Ⓓ grades

9. I'm going to take a _____ course so that my memos, letters, and reports are better.
- Ⓐ Customer Service
- Ⓑ Bookkeeping
- Ⓒ Public Speaking
- Ⓓ Business Writing

1 Ⓐ Ⓑ Ⓒ Ⓓ   4 Ⓐ Ⓑ Ⓒ Ⓓ   7 Ⓐ Ⓑ Ⓒ Ⓓ
2 Ⓐ Ⓑ Ⓒ Ⓓ   5 Ⓐ Ⓑ Ⓒ Ⓓ   8 Ⓐ Ⓑ Ⓒ Ⓓ
3 Ⓐ Ⓑ Ⓒ Ⓓ   6 Ⓐ Ⓑ Ⓒ Ⓓ   9 Ⓐ Ⓑ Ⓒ Ⓓ

Example:

Excuse me, Rosa. _____ help me?
- Ⓐ I can
- Ⓑ You can
- Ⓒ Can I
- ⬤ Can you

10. Sure. _____ help?
- Ⓐ How I can
- Ⓑ How you can
- Ⓒ How can I
- Ⓓ How can you

11. _____ how to turn on the alarm system?
- Ⓐ You can show me
- Ⓑ Can you show me
- Ⓒ I can show you
- Ⓓ Can I show you

12. Sure. _____
- Ⓐ I'll be happy.
- Ⓑ I'll be happy to.
- Ⓒ You'll be happy.
- Ⓓ You'll be happy to.

13. _____
- Ⓐ I see.
- Ⓑ That's correct.
- Ⓒ You're welcome.
- Ⓓ Thanks.

14. _____, close the door. _____, enter the code.
- Ⓐ Then . . . After that
- Ⓑ Then . . . First
- Ⓒ First . . . Then
- Ⓓ Finally . . . Then

15. _____
- Ⓐ I see.
- Ⓑ You see.
- Ⓒ Yes. That's correct.
- Ⓓ Excuse me.

16. _____, press ON. _____, leave the building.
- Ⓐ First . . . Then
- Ⓑ First . . . And finally
- Ⓒ After that . . . First
- Ⓓ After that . . . And finally

17. I press ON and leave the building. _____
- Ⓐ Can you help me?
- Ⓑ How can I help?
- Ⓒ Is that right?
- Ⓓ Are you right?

18. Yes. _____
- Ⓐ I'm correct.
- Ⓑ That's correct.
- Ⓒ Thanks very much.
- Ⓓ That isn't right.

10 Ⓐ Ⓑ Ⓒ Ⓓ 13 Ⓐ Ⓑ Ⓒ Ⓓ 16 Ⓐ Ⓑ Ⓒ Ⓓ
11 Ⓐ Ⓑ Ⓒ Ⓓ 14 Ⓐ Ⓑ Ⓒ Ⓓ 17 Ⓐ Ⓑ Ⓒ Ⓓ
12 Ⓐ Ⓑ Ⓒ Ⓓ 15 Ⓐ Ⓑ Ⓒ Ⓓ 18 Ⓐ Ⓑ Ⓒ Ⓓ

Go to the next page ▷

C READING: A Job Performance Evaluation

Look at this employee's job performance evaluation. Then do Numbers 19 through 22.

Employee Name ___Manuel Garcia___   Position ___Stock clerk___

	Excellent	Good	Needs Improvement	Unsatisfactory
The employee understands the job responsibilities.	✓			
The employee has the skills needed to do the job.		✓		
The employee communicates clearly.			✓	
The employee listens carefully to supervisors and co-workers.			✓	
The employee gets along well with co-workers.		✓		
The employee has a positive attitude.	✓			
The employee is dependable and hardworking.	✓			
The employee is polite and friendly with customers.				
The employee solves problems creatively.			✓	
The employee dresses appropriately.		✓		
The employee is well groomed.	✓			
The employee learns from feedback.			✓	
The employee continues to learn new skills.	✓			

Employee's Signature ___Manuel Garcia___   Date of Evaluation ___12/14/19___

Evaluated by (Print)___Larissa Silver___   Evaluator's Signature ___Larissa Silver___

19. The employee has _____ grades that are Excellent or Good.
   Ⓐ three
   Ⓑ five
   Ⓒ eight
   Ⓓ twelve

20. Larissa is Manuel Garcia's _____.
   Ⓐ supervisor
   Ⓑ stock clerk
   Ⓒ employee
   Ⓓ customer

21. We can infer that _____.
   Ⓐ the employee doesn't like his job
   Ⓑ the employee doesn't work hard
   Ⓒ the employee doesn't have very good listening and speaking skills
   Ⓓ the employee isn't dependable

22. One line of the evaluation form is not filled in. This is probably because _____.
   Ⓐ the employee isn't friendly with customers
   Ⓑ the employee isn't polite with customers
   Ⓒ customers complain about the employee
   Ⓓ the employee doesn't communicate with customers in his job

19 Ⓐ Ⓑ Ⓒ Ⓓ   20 Ⓐ Ⓑ Ⓒ Ⓓ   21 Ⓐ Ⓑ Ⓒ Ⓓ   22 Ⓐ Ⓑ Ⓒ Ⓓ

Look at the adult education catalog. Then do Numbers 23 through 26.

ADULT EDUCATION COURSES—FALL TERM

BUSINESS

BUS 101 Business Procedures—M, W, F
Learn the procedures in a business office. Topics include filing, telephone skills, receiving and sending mail, organizing meetings and conferences, scheduling appointments, making travel reservations, and time management.

BUS 105 Business Writing—M, W
This course helps students learn to write clear and concise business letters, memos, and reports.

BUS 201 Bookkeeping—M, Tu, W, Th, F
This course prepares students for the national Certified Bookkeeper examination. Topics include payroll (paying wages, reporting taxes) and inventory.

BUS 205 Entrepreneurship—W, F
Learn how to start and operate your own business. Each student will develop a business plan.

COMPUTERS

COM 101 Microsoft Word I—Tu, Th
Students will learn to create documents with the popular word processing software.

COM 102 Microsoft Outlook—F
Learn to use Microsoft Outlook to send, receive, and organize electronic mail.

COM 106 Excel Spreadsheets—Tu, Th
Balancing a checkbook and calculating family expenses is easier with Excel software. This course covers the basics of spreadsheets.

COM 201 Microsoft Word II—W, Th, F
Use the advanced features of Word to create documents with charts. Students will also learn to create newsletters and flyers.

COM 203 PowerPoint Presentations—M, F
Learn to create professional-looking presentations that include graphs, charts, and pictures using PowerPoint.

CULINARY ARTS

CA 100 Food Preparation—M, Tu, W, Th, F
Students learn kitchen procedures and basic recipes for an entry-level position as a Food and Beverage Specialist in a hotel, hospital, or restaurant kitchen.

CA 104 Food Sanitation—W, F
Learn how to prepare food safely. This course teaches health regulations and procedures and the reasons for them.

HEALTH SCIENCE

HS 101 CPR (Cardiopulmonary Resuscitation)—M
This course covers emergency procedures to follow when someone has stopped breathing or the heart has stopped beating. Red Cross certification.

---

23. Microsoft Word is software for _____.
    ⓐ giving presentations
    ⓑ sending and receiving e-mail
    ⓒ making spreadsheets
    ⓓ writing documents

24. Sonia and Mercedes are planning to start their own cleaning service company. They're going to take the course in _____ to prepare to open their business.
    ⓐ Entrepreneurship
    ⓑ Business Writing
    ⓒ CPR
    ⓓ Food Preparation

25. Julio can only take adult education courses on Tuesdays and Thursdays because of his work schedule. He's thinking about taking Course Number _____.
    ⓐ BUS 105
    ⓑ HS 101
    ⓒ COM 106
    ⓓ CA 100

26. Course Number _____ prepares students to take a national examination.
    ⓐ BUS 101
    ⓑ BUS 201
    ⓒ COM 106
    ⓓ CA 100

---

23 ⓐ ⓑ ⓒ ⓓ   24 ⓐ ⓑ ⓒ ⓓ   25 ⓐ ⓑ ⓒ ⓓ   26 ⓐ ⓑ ⓒ ⓓ

Go to the next page ⟶

E **CLOZE READING: A Promotion at Work**

Choose the correct answers to complete the memo.

CREATIVE COMPUTER SOLUTIONS

Interoffice Memorandum

TO: All Employees
FROM: Jane Hamilton, Director
SUBJECT: Promotion of Karima Mansoor

I am happy to announce the [evaluation (A) | promotion ● | education (C)] of Karima Mansoor to

the position of office manager. You all know that Karima has been doing an excellent job

as assistant manager. She's [hard work (A) | work hard (B) | hardworking (C)] ²⁷ and enthusiastic. She

[gets along (A) | knows (B) | takes care (C)] ²⁸ well with everyone in the office, she

[works (A) | communicates (B) | understands (C)] ²⁹ clearly, and she thinks [around (A) | inside (B) | outside (C)] ³⁰ the box

to find new ways to solve problems. Karima has recently finished a [grooming (A) | training (B) | solving (C)] ³¹

program that has prepared her well for this new position. She has completed a year of coursework in

[culinary (A) | sanitation (B) | business (C)] ³² procedures, and she has received the highest

[grades (A) | reports (B) | notes (C)] ³³ possible in this program. Karima's supervisor, Lidiya Sorreno, has given

Karima excellent job [appearance (A) | performance (B) | opportunity (C)] ³⁴ evaluations during the past three

years. Now that Lidiya has been promoted to the [position (A) | attitude (B) | evaluation (C)] ³⁵ of Director of

Personnel, we have decided that Karima is the best person to take Lidiya's place. We know that Karima

will do well with her new [supervisors (A) | responsibilities (B) | problems (C)] ³⁶. She has worked hard for our

company, and I know you agree that she [receives (A) | serves (B) | deserves (C)] ³⁷ this promotion.

---

27 Ⓐ Ⓑ Ⓒ Ⓓ   30 Ⓐ Ⓑ Ⓒ Ⓓ   33 Ⓐ Ⓑ Ⓒ Ⓓ   36 Ⓐ Ⓑ Ⓒ Ⓓ
28 Ⓐ Ⓑ Ⓒ Ⓓ   31 Ⓐ Ⓑ Ⓒ Ⓓ   34 Ⓐ Ⓑ Ⓒ Ⓓ   37 Ⓐ Ⓑ Ⓒ Ⓓ
29 Ⓐ Ⓑ Ⓒ Ⓓ   32 Ⓐ Ⓑ Ⓒ Ⓓ   35 Ⓐ Ⓑ Ⓒ Ⓓ

Go to the next page ⟶ **53**

LISTENING ASSESSMENT: Following a Sequence of Instructions

Read and listen to the questions. Then listen to the conversation and answer the questions.

38. When is the copy machine ready to print?
    - Ⓐ When the paper is regular size.
    - Ⓑ When the Start button is green.
    - Ⓒ When the lid is up.
    - Ⓓ When the green light is on.

39. What does the employee need to copy?
    - Ⓐ One regular-size page.
    - Ⓑ One large-size page.
    - Ⓒ Fifty regular-size pages.
    - Ⓓ Fifty large-size pages.

40. How can someone copy a large map on this machine?
    - Ⓐ Put it face down in the automatic document feeder.
    - Ⓑ Put it face up in the automatic document feeder.
    - Ⓒ Put it face down on the glass.
    - Ⓓ Put it face up on the glass.

G **WRITING ASSESSMENT: Your Education History & Education Plan**

Fill out the form. Write information about the schools you have attended, the skills you have, and your education plans for the future.

EDUCATION HISTORY

Dates _____   Degree or certificate _____

School, City, State _____

Dates _____   Degree or certificate _____

School, City, State _____

Dates _____   Degree or certificate _____

School, City, State _____

SKILLS

_____

EDUCATION PLANS FOR THE FUTURE

What you plan to study: _____   Where (Name or type of school): _____   When (Year): _____

H **SPEAKING ASSESSMENT**

I can ask and answer these questions:

Ask Answer
- ☐ ☐ Tell me about your skills.
- ☐ ☐ Tell me about your educational background.

Ask Answer
- ☐ ☐ What job do you want in the future?
- ☐ ☐ What new skills do you want to learn in the future?

STOP

38 Ⓐ Ⓑ Ⓒ Ⓓ   39 Ⓐ Ⓑ Ⓒ Ⓓ   40 Ⓐ Ⓑ Ⓒ Ⓓ

SIDE by SIDE *Plus* Test Prep Workbook 3 Audio Program

The *Side by Side Plus Test Prep Workbook 3* Digital Audio CD contains all listening activities in the unit achievement tests. Teachers can choose to do these activities in class or have students complete them on their own using the audio. The Digital Audio CD also includes MP3 files of the audio program for downloading to a computer or audio player.

Track	Activity
1	Introduction
2	Unit 1: p. 4 Exercise E
3	Unit 2: p. 9 Exercise F
4	Unit 3: p. 14 Exercise E
5	Unit 4: p. 17 Exercise F
6	Unit 5: p. 23 Exercise G
7	Unit 6: p. 29 Exercise F
8	Unit 7: p. 35 Exercise F
9	Unit 8: p. 41 Exercise F
10	Unit 9: p. 47 Exercise F
11	Unit 10: p. 54 Exercise F